Psychological Assessment
of Candidates
for a Religious Order

Charles A. Weisgerber, S.J.
University of Detroit

Loyola University Press
Chicago   60657

Cover photograph by Algimantas Kezys, S.J.

Imprimi potest Walter L. Farrell, S.J., Provincial of the
Detroit Province, July 22, 1968. *Nihil obstat* John B. Amberg,
S.J., *censor deputatus*, May 23, 1969. *Imprimatur* Right Rev-
erent Monsignor Francis W. Byrne, Vicar General, Archdiocese
of Chicago, May 26, 1969. The *nihil obstat* and *imprimatur*
are official declarations that a book or pamphlet is free of
doctrinal or moral error. No implication is contained therein
that those who have granted the *nihil obstat* and *imprimatur*
agree with the contents, opinions, or statements expressed.

Preface

THE use of psychological tests and methods in screening applicants to Catholic religious orders and diocesan seminaries has been going on for many years. Generally, it has been received with a certain amount of enthusiasm by the religious superiors, seminary rectors, and others who bear the responsibility of selection and training. Several meetings in recent years have demonstrated that a rather large number of psychologists are committed in some way to this work, all with basic faith in the value of what they are doing. Many are amassing an impressive amount of data and have plans ultimately to communicate their findings. A few have published a portion of their results. Some of the publications have provided evidence of modest success in the screening effort; some have given reasons for doubt. Very little is sufficiently detailed to aid others in developing their skills. Meanwhile, there have been superiors and vocation directors who have asked for proof that the selection of candidates is any better with the aid of psychological examination than without it.

Clearly, definitive answers are desired. This book does not pretend to give such answers, but it will help thereto. It presents the results with one segment of a religious order of men. The findings can be accepted with varying degrees of confidence. Generalizations have to be made with caution. However, the program herein described and evaluated has been in operation for some eighteen years; its study will be of help to others, even if it will do no more than provide them with hypotheses to check on their own data. And it is hoped that other psychologists will come forth with similar analyses, so that eventually we shall have a sufficient body of evidence on which to base definitive conclusions regarding the general effectiveness of the work and the choice and use of methods of assessment.

In embarking on the research, the author's first purpose was to prove to himself whether he was or was not doing an effective job. In publishing the results, he had in mind to sound a warning against the assumption—too readily made—that psychological techniques can be expected to solve all the problems of weeding out unfit candidates for the priesthood or the religious life. Meanwhile the program was continuing, and there was also an urgent need to determine the validity, for this specific purpose, of the tests and other instruments and to discover what scores, background factors, and the like might serve as diagnostic or predictive indicators. It had taken some ten years, and probably more mistakes than one would realize, to accumulate a modicum of such information. The account of these efforts is submitted in the hope that it will save the reader a considerable amount of time and make it possible for him to start his work at a higher level of skill or improve it faster. It will be up to his critical judgment and professional competence to decide which of the results are sufficiently well founded and can be applied to his own work.

From what has been said, it is obvious that this book is intended primarily for psychologists and others trained in personnel, clinical, or counseling work. Hence, the terminology is often quite technical. Nevertheless, it is hoped that many other people engaged in vocational work will also be able to see light through the fog and at least thread their way through Chapters 1, 2, and 11.

The very limited reference to the psychological literature does not imply lack of appreciation of what others have done it was the result of a decision to concentrate on the information that could be gleaned from this one program and to make it available. The reader who is interested in acquainting himself with the published material on screening of religious personnel and allied topics will do well to consult: Robert

J. Menges and James E. Dittes, *Psychological Stud' s of Clergymen* (New York: Thomas Nelson and Sons, 1965) and to look for periodic supplements in *Ministry Studies*, published by the Ministry Studies Board, 1717 Massachusetts Avenue, N.W., Washington, D.C. 20036.

Thanks are due to a number of men who have provided help in various ways: Reverends Robert C. Broome, Malcolm T. Carron, John R. Connery, Joseph F. Downey, Arthur K. Dugan, Walter L. Farrell, Robert F. Harvanek, Vincent V. Herr, Richard T. Malloy, John A. McGrail, Robert J. Murphy, Peter E. Nolan, Nicholas A. Predovich, Bernard J. Wernert, and perhaps again as many who on occasion gave of their time.

The following have graciously allowed me to reproduce in whole or in part material of theirs or under their copyright: Reverend William C. Bier, S.J.--his Sentence Completion Test and the description of his changes in the MMPI; Reverend Victor Anthony Coelho, S.J.--his M.A. thesis; Reverend Harry C. Meserve, D.D. and the Academy of Religion and Mental Health--an article of mine in the *Journal of Religion and Health*; and Dr. Frederick C. Thorne, editor and publisher--an article in the *Journal of Clinical Psychology*. To them my sincere thanks.

Charles A. Weisgerber, S.J.
University of Detroit
June 20, 1969

Note

References are indicated in the text by citing author and date; the full information is given in the *References* at the end of each chapter. These sections also serve as bibliography.

TABLE OF CONTENTS

Chapter 1

Description of Program

THE main purpose of this book is to report research on
psychological screening for a religious order of men. The
order has novitiates in various parts of the country. This
report concerns men who have applied for admission to two
novitiates in the Midwest. The program has been in operation
since 1950.

Procedures

Had the screening been originally conceived as solely
a research project, the methods would have been fixed at
the beginning and kept constant throughout. One would then
need to give no more than a relatively brief description of
these procedures. However, it was intended to provide service and was subject to revision in the light of experience.
Hence it is necessary to detail the various changes that
have been made in order that the reader may have a clear
picture of the changing basis of the research.

All religious orders have some way of evaluating those who seek admission. The basic method used in this order has been standardized for generations, if not for centuries. The candidate is first seen by a priest whose position amounts to that of a local vocation director who takes care of assembling the necessary documents and guiding the young man through the various stages of the admission process. He has the responsibility of determining the man's fitness from the spiritual, moral, and canonical standpoints. Ideally he will have a number of interviews while he explores and tests the vocational aims of the candidate, his motivation, knowledge of the religious life, background, spiritual development, the firmness of his decision, and so on. Sometimes, by force of circumstances, one or two such meetings must suffice. In cases of obvious unfitness or unreadiness, he will not permit the applicant to proceed further but will advise him that he does not appear to have a vocation, or that he should defer his application for the time being. His norms are the classical principles of spiritual direction, his own experience in this work, and his practical knowledge of human behavior. There is thus some preliminary screening at the start, although it is not professionally psychological. If he thinks the candidate is probably or possibly fit, he sends him to three other priests, who interview him once. These use a similar method of approach and similar norms, although some are now trained psychologists. The content of these interviews is also specified by certain norms derived from canon law and the constitutions of the order, but considerable latitude is given for further exploration. There are thus four men in all, technically called examiners, each of whom makes an independent judgment regarding fitness and reports directly to the major superior.

It should be noted also that in very many cases these men will have known the candidate for some time, if he comes from a school or parish in which they are working. In other instances, inquiry is made of persons given as references. Gradually a reference form was developed and made use of with all applicants (cf. Appendix A). This form had, some time before the initiation of the psychological screening, been structured as a rough rating scale, covering a number of significant aspects of health, personality, and behavior. Of more recent vintage were the following requirements: a medical examination, transcripts of high school and college credits, the A.C.E. Psychological Examination (College Level, 1944 Form), the Cooperative English Test, Mechanics of Expression (Form A), and a privately standardized Latin test.

The psychological screening began rather modestly and on a trial basis with the addition of Bier's 1949 revision of the Minnesota Multiphasic Personality Inventory (MMPI), the use of the previously mentioned rating form with all candidates, and the assignment of a psychologist to the task of evaluating this material. (For a description of Bier's revision, see Chapter 3 and Appendix B.) The tests were administered by the local vocation director. The candidates were asked to designate three men, belonging to the same order whenever possible, who would know them best; and the rating forms were sent to these men. When these forms were returned, the psychologist was given them, the MMPI, and a summary containing the scores of the other tests, grade averages, and IQs derived from the high-school entrance test (the Henmon-Nelson for most of them).

Upon studying this material, the psychologist made a judgment on the fitness of the candidates, primarily from the standpoint of mental health. Those who were simply passed were not seen by the psychologist. When there was doubt about fitness, he interviewed them and gave further tests if feasible; if not, he had another psychologist give the tests and conduct an interview. Generally the Thematic Apperception Test, the Rorschach, and the Draw-a-Person Test were used. The protocols and notes concerning the interview were sent to the first psychologist, who made the interpretation and the final judgment on the personality of the candidate. This judgment consisted in declaring the man satisfactory, doubtful, or unsatisfactory, although these verbal distinctions were not formalized until the second year of operation. At first, little, if any, comment was added if the subject was thought satisfactory; if he was thought doubtful or unsatisfactory, an explanation was given and a rather full report of the findings of the further tests. In subsequent years, that is, from 1952 on, a brief personality description was given, even for those declared satisfactory. The report always included a recommendation of acceptance or other appropriate action. In a few cases psychiatric examination was suggested.

For the first year it was agreed that the MMPI was to be used only experimentally and that no decision to reject an applicant was to be made on the basis of this test alone. However, the records available to the writer seem to indicate that this restriction did not apply to the further tests and interview; some applicants were rejected or told to wait a year on the basis of this further information. Although this practice is defensible from a humane standpoint, it has served to reduce the validity of the writer's subsequent research because these unfavorable predictions of the psy-

3

chologist could not be put to the test of confirmation or refutation by the candidate's behavior in the religious life.

For five years the procedure remained essentially the same, the only important change being an increase in the number of references to include all members of the order who had taught the candidate in his last two years of school. However, some other revisions were in the making when, in 1955, illness of the psychologist forced the virtual suspension of the program. For applicants in this year, the tests were given as usual, but they were not to be used further unless there was some doubt of fitness on other grounds. The writer was appointed to take over the screening as of the following year. However, as an afterthought he was sent many of the MMPIs and ratings of those who applied for admission. Reports were made on these latter men; but many had already been accepted, and there was no opportunity to follow up the rest by further tests or interview. At the end of the year, an attempt was made to get all of the MMPIs, but a number had by that time been lost. With future research in mind, the author made a judgment on the basis of this test, but with little confidence in his opinion because of the lack of other information. For the most part, this class has been excluded from the studies reported in this book, except when the focus was solely on the MMPI. For research purposes, the classes of 1950–1954 comprise a coherent group and are best studied separately from the rest, especially in view of the changes in procedure to be detailed below.

In 1955 Bier had made a further revision of the MMPI, and this was adopted for subsequent classes. A Sentence Completion Test, designed by Bier, was added (see Appendix D). (A revision was made by the writer in 1957 and adopted in 1958; it is reproduced in Chapter 6.) The A.C.E. was discontinued in 1957 and replaced by the School and College Ability Test (SCAT), Form 1A (see Chapter 7). More recently still, this was also dropped from the routine battery because today's high-school and college students are usually rather overtested in the ability sphere. The SCAT is used only if ability is not clear from a combination of grades and such tests as the Scholastic Aptitude Test of the College Entrance Examination Board, the battery of the American College Testing Program, and the like. The Cooperative English and the Latin Achievement tests have long been discontinued. The Modern Language Aptitude Test (Carroll & Sapon, 1959), which is also predictive of success in Latin, has for several years been used when the applicant has been weak in Latin or has had none at all. Instead of the summary of grades, a transcript of high-school and college work is provided. The Allport-Vernon-Lindzey Study of Values was used experimentally for three years (see Chapter 8).

4

The most changed instrument has been the rating form, which originally was somewhat jejune and quite vulnerable to the "halo effect." An extensive revision was introduced in 1955. It contained 38 traits to be rated on a five-point scale, a space for indicating the person's outstanding characteristic, an overall rating of fitness for the religious life, and a request for a brief personality description and other pertinent information. Although the form could have been used psychometrically by averaging ratings, this was not done. The personality description and background information was the part that proved really helpful: in fact, often indispensable. After a number of complaints about the difficulty of making the ratings and the author's firsthand observation of the results of imposing such a task on men unsophisticated in the ways of rating scales, an adjective checklist was substituted (1957), and fuller directions were given for the personality sketch, which was to include: family background, school history, spiritual development, social life, motivation, maturity, stability, range of intellectual interests, sense of humor, and so on. The checklist was meant mainly to "prime" the respondent for the personality description. As of 1967, a form is used which was modelled on that developed by the Peace Corps. Besides these variations in form, the policy regarding choice of reference persons has also changed. In very many cases these may be teachers, employers, and the like, who are not members of the order. Their number is also variable although it is usually from four to six.

From both clinical and research standpoints any such source of information poses problems. The amount and accuracy of the information is quite variable from case to case. The informants tend generally to be rather benign in their judgments, and for this reason one attends more to the facts they recount than to the conclusions they draw from them. College teachers usually have little more than superficial knowledge of the applicants. Teachers in schools not conducted by male religious are often but dimly aware of the nature of the religious life and the special stresses of the novitiate and years of training. This is particularly true of lay teachers, unless they are ex-seminarians or ex-religious. It is clear, then, that the information available to the psychologist ranges from comparatively little to a rather full picture; hence, his chances of successful prediction vary. In this respect, however, we may risk anticipating the data by pointint out that no single assessment tool seems sufficient by itself; but now one, now the other supplies critical information which prevents a serious error.

Mention must also be made of an autobiography, which has been used since 1961. This is generally written at home. The instructions are purposely somewhat vague, so as to leave the candidate free to select what he thinks is important. He is told merely to write an autobiography of 500-1000 words, covering the persons or experiences in the course of his development that stand out in his mind as having most influence in making him the kind of person he is, and, lastly, the development of his vocation. It is relatively brief because even 500 words seem like a long assignment to many at the high-school or early college age. No formal method of analysis of the content is attempted. In a qualitative way, it provides information on background and motivation, although caution must be exercised in taking the account at face value.

Another source of information has for some years been available, but only for one sub-group of candidates. The four priest-examiners referred to previously are asked to append to their formal report a page in which they describe in some detail their impression of the candidate's personality, background, motivation, and the like. A summary is made of these by the superior's assistant and sent to the psychologist. This has proved to be quite valuable.

One of the last bits of advice given the writer by his predecessor was to have all the candidates interviewed by a psychologist. This policy was adopted in 1957 and has been followed since then, with some rare exceptions forced by circumstances--and occasionally with subsequent regrets. The plan was to assign to the task one psychologist in each of the colleges operated by the order in the geographical area from which the candidates generally come. However, from 1958 on, the writer has been doing the interviewing himself in about forty per cent of the cases. The cooperating psychologists have the following information at their disposal: ratings, transcripts, and the writer's report, including some suggestions of things to inquire about particularly. The latter may be specific responses in the MMPI and the Sentence Completion Test, or such things as motivation, indecision, family relations, and so on. Further tests may be recommended. As to the general form of the interview, they are asked to follow the line of questioning suggested for a diagnostic interview in the textbooks on psychiatry or clinical psychology. No specifications are given concerning the form of the report, since that is left up to them as responsible professional persons. Some give brief reports; some, a very detailed and interpretive description.

The author himself commonly begins the interview by going over a number of responses in the MMPI and occasionally the

Sentence Completion Test. Then he covers the areas of development and present functioning indicated, for example, in Strecker, Ebaugh, and Ewalt (1947). Unless the information is already available, the candidate is also questioned regarding scrupulosity, motivation, the development of the vocation idea, definiteness of the decision, what aspects of the novitiate appear most difficult and what easiest. The length of the interview varies from about 45 minutes to about 1 1/2 hours. Occasionally further tests are given. The Rorschach and Thematic Apperception Test are hardly ever used because the writer has found that, if he cannot make up his mind by the end of the interview, these tests will not help him do so. On occasion there is need for a test of intelligence, reading, and so on.

Up to this point we have been speaking of the screening of candidates ultimately destined for the priesthood. Those who wish to become brothers have also been examined since 1956. For them the process is essentially the same, except that they have not been given either achievement or college-aptitude tests. In place of the latter, the Army General Classification Test, First Civilian Edition has been used. The brothers show a wider range of talent, age, and experience; hence, a test was desired which would provide a comparison with the general population. This test also has norms for college entrance and can be scored separately for its three parts: vocabulary, arithmetic, and blocks (spatial visualization and reasoning); these scores can be used later, when the brothers are given a battery of special tests. (For a description of this program see Chapter 10.)

Overview of the Current Procedures

The detailing of the various changes and modifications in procedure has been necessary for a clear picture of the shifting basis of the psychologist's decisions, which must be kept in mind throughout the subsequent reports of follow-up research. Attention will be called to some of these details in connection with specific research problems. But now the reader may wish to have a summary account of the process as it exists currently.

At about the same time that the candidate is seen by the four examiners required by rule, as explained at the beginning of this chapter, the rating forms are sent out to at least four and preferably about six persons who are thought to know him well. Bier's MMPI (1955 version) and the Sentence Completion Test are given by the first examiner, according to directions specified by the writer. The SCAT and Modern Language Aptitude Test are used in some cases, as

7

previously indicated; the Army General Classification Test, with brother candidates. Transcripts are obtained from the high schools and colleges attended. A medical examination is arranged. The autobiography is written at home or in one of the testing sessions. The psychologist receives the tests, ratings, transcripts, and autobiography. For one sub-group he also gets a summary of the comments of the four examiners and, in most cases, the medical report. This is the ideal situation; in practice there are often delays and emergencies which make it necessary to go on to the next step before all of these materials are in.

The psychologist first analyzes the tests because he prefers to obtain an impression on the basis of the tests, independently of the other information. In the MMPI, besides profile analysis, certain critical items are checked, as also the responses to the items in some of the scales which are highest in the profile. The Sentence Completion Test is not scored, but used in a qualitative fashion; it usually provides information (all of which must, of course, be taken tentatively) about home life, motivation, attitude to life and associates, and the like. Then come the autobiography, the transcript, the ratings, the summary of the impressions of the four official examiners, and the medical report. Lastly, he prepares his tentative report, if the man is to be interviewed by another psychologist, or makes note of things to look for himself if he is to be the interviewer. In the latter case, he also rates the candidate as satisfactory, doubtful, or unsatisfactory, so that later he will be able to distinguish his rating after the interview from his impression based only on the tests and other "paper" information. The final report of the writer takes this form: The candidate is first classed as satisfactory, doubtful, or unsatisfactory; then a personality description is written and various strengths or weaknesses are discussed; lastly, a recommendation is made regarding acceptance or some other course of action. The description is generally comparatively brief, about a half-page. It serves a dual purpose: to give the superior the reasons for the rating, and to aid the master of novices in his early counseling and guidance of the candidate.

Some Further Questions

A question has often been asked about referral to a psychiatrist. In one metropolitan area a psychiatrist now conducts the follow-up interview. Otherwise it is rare that psychiatric consultation is called for. Perhaps the program is open to criticism on this score, but the writer has usually found that, if he is uncertain about the fitness of a candidate, the psychiatrist is equally uncertain--perhaps because both have difficulty drawing a line between the dubiously fit and the dubiously unfit.

In the beginning, the primary purpose of the screening was to detect mental-health risks. Gradually its scope was enlarged to include psycho-social adjustment, acceptance of rules and authority, motivation, firmness of decision, and so on. Very early it was seen that the psychological findings would be helpful in counseling the novices; in fact, that was the initial reason for giving a personality description. However, the primary intent of the program remains screening, not counseling. There are good reasons for this. In the first place, canon law, the constitutions of the order, formal policy decisions of higher superiors, and papal documents stress the need for careful selection of religious and seminarians from the beginning. Secondly, upon entrance, the young religious acquires some rights which he did not have before, and these grow stronger as he advances beyond the novitiate; he has a tie to the order which requires a more definite and compelling reason for dismissing him than would have been demanded for simply not admitting him. Further, papal pronouncements (Pius XII, 1958) have called attention to the right of the individual to privacy in his psychic life, and some moral theologians and canonists question the right of superiors to require psychological tests or psychiatric examinations of any religious, even novices. Indeed, a former head of this order had made it quite clear that none of his religious should be compelled to take such tests. From the standpoint of the good of the applicant, it is certainly kinder to him in the long run to refuse admission because of serious doubts about his fitness than to expose him to risk of a breakdown or the painful readjustment if he has to leave the order later.

Research Subjects

The greater bulk of the research concerns candidates destined ultimately for the priesthood. Since those who chose to enter as brothers were not included at the beginning of the testing program and were smaller in numbers, comparatively little research was devoted to them. Occasionally a man decides in the novitiate or later that he wishes to be a brother rather than a priest. When such a change was made, the man was counted with the brother group.

The classes are designated by year of entry to the novitiate, although in many cases the testing was done a year or even two years earlier. In some instances the tests or merely the psychological interview had been repeated; the second test or the second report, as the case may be, was the one used in the research. As has been indicated previously, the first group that figures in the follow-up is comprised of the first five classes, 1950-1954. The 1955 class has been omitted from most of the studies for the reasons previously given. The research is then resumed with 1956 and, for the most part, carried to 1962. However, various studies involved various subgroups, the reason being often a matter of circumstances. The brother group entered in 1956-1963. The work on the Study of Values (Chapter 8) involved the 1962-1964 entrants.

The subjects are, of course, all male. The writer has no accurate statistics on the number who had applied to this order in these years because there were always some who were excluded or withdrew before it came time to give the tests or send them to the psychologist. In a preliminary survey, an attempt had been made to include those who had been rejected, deferred, or had spontaneously withdrawn. However, this attempt was abandoned, with the exception of the study of "hits" and "bad misses" in Chapters 3 and 10, as well as the analysis of the Sentence Completion Test in Chapter 6. Some data are certainly lost by the decision to include only those who actually entered the novitiate. This is particularly true when there is some external confirmation of an adverse judgment rendered by the psychologist. But we shall discuss this question more fully later.

The number of candidates admitted are as follows:

For the priesthood   For the brotherhood

1950-1954	211		
1955	47		
1956-1962	415	1956-1963	83
Total	673		

The figures given later for specific studies will not always add up to these totals. The work on various questions was done at different times over a period of years and could not readily be brought up to date for the present writing. At the time, it was frequently necessary to drop cases because the follow-up information had not yet come in and the research could not be delayed further. Often, too, subjects had to be excluded because of the nature of the study, because the wrong form of the MMPI was used, and so on. The various reasons will be indicated later, as appropriate.

The men in question were admitted to novitiates of the order in the Midwest. Most of them were born and raised in this area, or at least resided there at the time of entry;

10

comparatively few were at the time living in other parts of the country. It would be possible to specify the numbers state-by-state, but this hardly appears sufficiently pertinent. The vast majority came from large cities; an appreciable number, from smaller cities and towns; very few, from strictly rural areas.

Socioeconomic background is never considered in admissions, except in as far as it pertains to the son's obligation to aid his parents. Nor is there sufficient inquiry to make it possible to classify the men according to any of the conventional scales of socioeconomic status. However, their families would be considered middle class for the most part, with very few in the higher- or lower-income groups. They are white, except for one Negro and one Tanganyikan of Goan ancestry. Almost all are at least second-generation Americans; only a few are foreign born.

As to educational level, none of the candidates for the priesthood are admitted before graduation from high school; a large number have some college; some have completed college; a few have taken some graduate or professional studies; and an occasional one has the M.A., the Ph.D., or Ll.B. The level of the brothers is not quite this high, although only rarely is one admitted without a high-school diploma. The ability level is generally very high, as will be seen in Chapters 7 and 10. To give only the figures for the SCAT sample, the mean scaled scores were: Verbal 309.8 (S.D.: 11.2); Quantitative: 320.4 (S.D.: 12.7); Total: 314.4 (S.D.: 10.3). The vast majority had held some part-time or summer jobs; some had worked a year or more before entrance. Of the brother candidates, an appreciable number had held good jobs for some years, while a few were in rather responsible positions.

Statistics on age have been computed for the 1956-1962 classes and are representative enough of the whole group (cf. Chapter 4). The mean is 19.09; median, 18.13; mode, 18; S.D., 2.72; range, 16 (one case)--40 (one case). Actually, only a small number are older than 24 at the time of admission. These are for the candidates to the priesthood. A higher proportion of the brothers would be appreciably older, although mean, median, and mode would be about the same as for the rest.

References

Carroll, John B. and Stanley M. Sapon. *Modern Language Aptitude Test, Manual*. 1959 Edition. New York: Psychological Corporation, 1959.

Pius XII, Pope. "Applied Psychology." Address to the Rome Congress of the International Association of Applied Psychology, April 10, 1958. (Translated by N.C.W.C. News Service.) Washington, D.C.: National Catholic Welfare Conference, n.d.

Strecker, Edward A., Franklin G. Ebaugh, and Jack R. Ewalt. *Practical Clinical Psychiatry*. Sixth edition. Philadelphia: Blakiston, 1947. pp. 19-24.

Chapter 2

General Evaluation of the Program

Oₙ the research agenda, first place clearly belongs to
a general evaluation of the success of the psychological
screening program. Although a good case can be made theoretically for waiting still further, that is, until these
men have been engaged long enough in the actual work of the
priesthood to obtain a measure of their success in their
life's work, practically it is imperative to determine
whether the screening is effective or not. Religious superiors and others concerned with the admission of prospective
novices need to know whether and to what extent they can
rely on the professional help of the psychologist in assessing the fitness of the young men whose future they have to
decide.

Their concern, of course, is not the technical details
of the tests and other selection instruments but the overall judgment regarding the psychological health of the applicants. To this we shall direct our attention in this
chapter. As has been indicated, the psychologist in charge
of the program we are studying rated each candidate as

13

satisfactory, doubtful, or unsatisfactory. The primary emphasis was on mental health, but general adjustment and the likelihood of perseverance were also considered.

Obtaining adequate criterion information is of major importance, and the problems in this regard have led to the decision to restrict the research, for the most part, to those who entered the novitiate. For those who were not admitted, the information in the files was sufficient in only a few cases each year. For example, some candidates are accepted but withdraw before the entrance day arrives and often enough at the last minute. Such behavior may be due to indecision or instability, and to include these men in the study is tempting. But they do not always give more than a superficial or vague reason for their change of heart, so that it is impossible to be sure in most cases whether they had good cause to withdraw or merely did not have the courage to go through with their commitment. In a few instances a breakdown, some form of maladjustment, or other undesirable behavior later occurred and came to the writer's attention. There were also some who entered another order or the diocesan seminary and were successful. But to include only the handful of cases in which enough information is available would pose the risk of biasing the results. It would not be impossible to contact most of the men and interview them or have them fill out a questionnaire, but the value of the information would be debatable. If the psychologist judges a man unsuited, he means this with reference to life in the order. If the man functions well in the lay state, the diocesan seminary, or even another order, the prediction is not proved wrong, since the conditions of life are not the same. Nor, if the judgment had been favorable, does adequate functioning in the lay state prove anything. One cannot even absolutely rule out the possibility that poor adjustment to lay life would not necessarily imply the same in religious life, although the odds are heavy against this possibility. Hence, the writer is of the opinion that, even with adequate follow-up information on those who did not enter the novitiate, one could not be sure of its meaning.

Most of those denied admission are not simply rejected but are told to wait a year or two. About 80 per cent of these are not heard from again, and they may perhaps be classed as equivalently dropouts. However, many of them take deferral as a polite rejection or as indication that they do not have a vocation; and some, of course, fall in love or get wrapped up in some line of social service or the lay apostolate. Hence, it is doubtful whether inclusion of these men in the research would add anything but greater error. Still, in some few cases, there is sufficient evidence of unfitness for the religious life; these have been included in one phase of the ensuing studies. And, in the work on the Sentence Completion Test, described in Chapter 6, it was possible to include almost all of those who applied. As a rule, it seems better to restrict one's attention to those who actually entered, even though one is losing some data and probably biasing the results against the screening program to some degree.

There is another difficulty that works against the chances of getting clearly favorable results: the fact that some screening takes place even before the psychological tests are given. As indicated in Chapter 1, when the candidate first applies, he is sent to one man whose duty it is to make a preliminary assessment and decide whether there is sufficient indication of a true vocation to justify continuing the admission process. Although he is not a psychologist, he will have had considerable experience with adolescents and will be alert to marked deviations from the normal in behavior, mood, attitudes, and so on. Further, since the majority of the candidates come from one of the schools staffed by the order, the examiner often will be fairly well acquainted with the young man already, or some counselor in the school may have equivalently done the preliminary screening. If he looks promising enough, the candidate is then interviewed by three other men who have a similar background in professional experience. In the first few years of the program, the psychological tests were not given until four examiners, then, had been heard from and the verdict had been that at least there was enough in favor of the candidate to justify proceeding. Hence, the psychological assessment involved a group which had already been screened to some extent. This leads to the difficulty one usually experiences in evaluating a testing program with a comparatively select group.

The criteria employed were: perseverance vs. dropping out, mental health, overall adjustment to the religious life, and--for those in the first three years of the program--ordination to the priesthood. The first is analagous to the success-fail criterion which is frequently used in evaluating selection procedures. It has the advantage of being objective. It has also been criticized, particularly on the score that to leave the religious life is often no more than a manly, mature recognition of a lack of vocation and an error--perhaps a very immature, emotional decision-- in entering the novitiate in the first place. This point is probably well taken, and it can be pressed vigorously when

15

the viewpoint is that of mental health. However, even in this regard leaving the religious life after vows is almost always preceded by some emotional problem, unless the reason is simply failure in studies or poor health: i.e., truly physical and not either psychosomatic or hypochondriac. And from the standpoint of adjustment, given the same proviso as above, it argues some failure which would at least involve the classification of "simple maladjustment" in the older psychiatric terminology. With those who leave in the novitiate, one would not perhaps press the concept of maladjustment to the same extent; but it seems clear that candidates do not leave unless they feel they don't belong and, therefore, are not subjectively well adjusted to the religious life. The experience may or may not have done them some good; but, from the standpoint of the order, they have not realized the hope with which they were admitted and have proved objectively unsatisfactory candidates or at least doubtful. To return to those who leave after vows, superiors will tell you that only very rarely is there no evidence of a social, emotional, or behavior problem.

To obtain information regarding mental health and overall adjustment in preparation of the study reported earlier (Weisgerber, 1962), a quasi rating form was used. This was not a scale in the strict sense, but rather a convenient method of collecting the desired information in a consistent manner. The purpose was primarily to identify those who have proved unsatisfactory or doubtful. The form is reproduced here.

Rating on _____ By_____

Mental Health[1]

5   Hospitalized, left, and/or sent home because of mental illness or impending mental illness.

4   Has been or is under psychiatric or psychological treatment.

3   Has had or has illness ostensibly physical but diagnosed as psychosomatic, i.e., primarily due to emotional difficulties.

2   Tense, nervous, anxious, moody, emotional, hypochondriac, or similar trouble.

1   No emotional difficulties of any significance.

?   Don't know.

Details (such as nature of trouble, duration, treatment, outcome, and so forth):

_____

_____

16

Discipline
__3__ Rebellious, troublemaker, very poor observer, and/
    or very irresponsible.
__2__ In between.
__1__ Good observer, no trouble.
__?__ Don't know.

Social Adjustment (with classmates and co-workers):
__3__ Doesn't get along, quarrelsome, uncooperative,
    unadaptable.
__2__ In between.
__1__ Well liked, cooperative, respected, a leader.
__?__ Don't know.

Adequacy of Work
As student (as to effort rather than ability or actual
success):
__3__ Lazy, uninterested, negligent.
__2__ In between.
__1__ Above average for hard work, diligence, interest.
__?__ Don't know.
As teacher (and in other functions such as extracurric-
lars):
__3__ Not really interested, neglectful, gets by with
    minimum.
__2__ In between.
__1__ Devoted, very interested, faithful, very cooper-
    ative.
__?__ Don't know.

If he has left the Order, reason for leaving (in as far
as you know and are permitted to say):

_____

_____

Date of leaving _____

An attempt was made to limit the statements in the form
as much as possible to things which are a matter of objective record, or at least to behavior which would require a minimum of subjective interpretation.

Information on most of the subjects was obtained from
two men. The reason for this number was that in the periodic reviews of the young religious during their training after the novitiate two men are actually the primary
and most reliable sources of information: the official
responsible for discipline and the one responsible for
their work, usually the dean. When, as happened in some

cases, it was not feasible to get information from both these supervisors, recourse was had to a teacher, a local superior, or to the records of the major superior. When two ratings could not be obtained, the subjects in question were excluded from this phase of the research,[2] except for those who left the order during the novitiate. For them the master of novices was the only source. This was not merely a matter of convenience. The master of novices has a conference with each man at least once a month. While others, particularly his assistant, will have about as much opportunity as he for external observation, they will ordinarily not have the intimate contact with them involved in these conferences. Hence it appeared safer to rely on the novice master solely, as a sort of qualified witness, rather than to run the risk of mixing superficial information with the more penetrating. Nor did it seem justifiable simply to exclude these cases, because this would introduce a serious bias in the results.

There was some risk from the standpoint of confidentiality. However, this had been worked out in previous follow-up. The solution agreed upon was that it would be left to his judgment as to what could be communicated to a professional person for professional purposes. It was understood that anything in the nature of conscience matter was excluded and that the writer would not ask further questions. Similarly, the "spiritual father" later responsible for the guidance of the young religious would in many cases have been the best source of reliable information in regard to emotional problems and reasons for leaving after the novitiate. However, because his position is exclusively that of spiritual director, it seemed that there was simply too much risk, and that it would be practically impossible for him to say anything without getting into conscience matter. This is so important a consideration that the research simply had to suffer.

After the information was collated, the subjects were classified by the writer as satisfactory, doubtful, or unsatisfactory, first in regard to mental health and secondly in regard to overall judgment. The ideal research procedure would have been to have this done by another psychologist. However, confidentiality again enters the picture, and the writer did not feel he could permit anyone else to see the records. To reduce the margin of subjectivity, he prepared specific guidelines for the classification, which are reproduced here.

Mental Health alone:
Unsatisfactory: 1) 5* (either rater), or
2) 3 or 4 (either rater) and left order, or
3) Breakdown in subsequent history (after leaving).
Doubtful: 1) 3 or 4 (either rater) and still in order, or
2) 2 (either rater) and left, or
3) Indecision, emotional problem, very odd.
Satisfactory: All others.

*These numbers refer to the code numbers that stand for the items on the rating sheet checked by the informants.

Overall Adjustment:
Unsatisfactory: 1) Unsatisfactory in mental health, or
2) Any 3 (either rater) and left, or
3) Dismissed (or equivalent) or left after vows were put off, or
4) Serious emotional problem was reason for leaving.
Doubtful: 1) Doubtful in mental health, or
2) Any 3 (either rater; and second rater not more than one point off) and still in, or
3) MH 2 (either rater) and left, or
4) Reason for leaving or novitiate behavior indicative of: immaturity, indecision, instability of purpose, lack of seriousness of purpose, failure to give it a try, or failure to estimate the life in advance, or
5) Subsequent history showing indecision.
Satisfactory: All others.

Note—"MH" means mental health. The equivalent of dismissal means that, although the man left voluntarily, he was told to go or pressure was applied. "Any 3" means a 3 in any category, i.e., mental health, discipline, social adjustment, or adequacy of work.

The fact of leaving the order figures in the classification, as is evident in numerous cases above. The reasons for this may be illustrated by considering the #2 rating under the heading of mental health: i.e., "tense, nervous, anxious, moody, emotional, hypochondriac, or similar trouble." If a young man was so designated, he was counted as satisfactory if he persevered, doubtful, if he left. The thinking was that this kind of trouble was not sufficiently significant in itself but that leaving the order indicated that eventually he could not tolerate the condition or reduce it enough to live with it in the religious life. One can probably quarrel with such an argument. Perhaps the role of leaving in the classification accounts in part for the fact, which will be seen later, that there is no great discrepancy between results for mental health or overall adjustment and those obtained by applying the criterion of perseverance versus leaving. However, it is unlikely that it biased the data against rather than for the screening program.

Mental health was regarded of major importance; hence, no one found doubtful or unsatisfactory in this domain received any better rating for overall adjustment. Some novices did not stay long enough to permit any judgment in regard to mental health. These were omitted from the mental health data.

Results--1950-1954 Classes

Our first consideration is the classes represented in the 1962 study. The entire group numbered 211, after the exclusion of one who belonged to a foreign-language mission and one who had been readmitted later. However, there were 12 for whom the records still available did not clearly indicate whether the psychologist's report was favorable or unfavorable, and three for whom no test or report could be found. Rather than merely summarize the earlier study here, the results have been brought up to date. No further rating forms were sent out. However, a check was made on those who subsequently left by getting the major superior to indicate the reason for leaving. Further, except for the last class, most of the men had reached the point of ordination. Since presentation to the ordaining bishop requires a careful scrutiny by superiors, the fact that a man was approved for ordination and went through with it amounted to another favorable rating on him. This worked out rather fortunately, since it enabled the retrieval of many cases previously excluded because of difficulty getting a second rating: those particularly who were sent to the foreign missions and usually must be counted among the best men. Still, as in the previous study, the total number of cases is not the same in the various tables because of differences in the adequacy of the information.

Table 2.1 shows the results according to the criterion of mental health.

Table 2.1

Success of Predictions against Criterion of Mental Health

A Expressed in Numbers

Prediction	Outcome Satisfactory	Doubtful	Unsatisfactory	Total
Satisfactory	125	30	11	166
Doubtful	16	8	3	27
Unsatisfactory	2			2
Total*	147	42	15	204

B Expressed in Percentages

Prediction	Satisfactory	Doubtful	Unsatisfactory	Total
Satisfactory	75.3	18.1	6.6	100.0
Doubtful	59.3	29.6	11.1	100.0
Unsatisfactory	100.0			100.0
Total*	72.1	20.6	7.4	100.1

Summary Statistics: C = .106; γ = .371; χ^2 = 2.210; d.f. = 1; P = .20   (Chi square computed from 2 x 2 table.)

* Includes those not tested or for whom the psychologist's judgment could not be ascertained with certainty. And so for the other tables in this section.

In this instance, the data are presented a little more fully than later, the percentages being given in detail here and more summarily later. This is by way of illustration. The totals for the columns include those not tested or for whom the records did not clearly indicate the psychologist's judgment. This is done here and in the following tables so that the reader can see the so-called base rate, that is, the number or percentage actually coming under a certain classification regardless of how the psychologist had originally marked them. The figures called "summary statistics" also need explanation. C is Cramér's statistic: γ is an index suggested by Goodman and Kruskal to assess predictive value.[3] A constant difficulty with the data is the small number in the unsatisfactory category. Again and again, χ^2 cannot be computed without compressing the table, often into 2 x 2 form, as in this instance.

Before discussing these results, a comment must be made regarding the use of any sort of sampling statistics with the data at hand. This group is not a sample, but the whole population for the five classes except for those excluded for good reasons, unconnected with sampling theory. There are only two ways in which the group can be considered a sample: (1) if it is taken as part of the whole run of candidates from the beginning of the screening program to the present and future classes, and (2) if it is taken to represent candidates for other novitiates of the same order or male religious orders in general. In either case, however, it is not a random sample. The statistical indices presented here, and elsewhere in this book, are of descriptive use only. Statements are made regarding statistical significance or probability simply because the technically sophisticated reader will be looking for them. Any generalizations based on the data must be taken as informed hypotheses to be tested by replication.

Tables 2.2--2.4 present the results with the criteria of overall adjustment, perseverance, and ordination respectively. For the last, six cases had to be excluded because, while the rest of their original classes have been ordained, they have been delayed of their own choice or because of doctoral work in their speciality before beginning their theology.

Table 2.2

Success of Predictions against Criterion of Overall Adjustment

Outcome

Prediction	Satis.	Doubt.	Unsat.	Total	% Satis.
Satisfactory	97	39	32	168	57.7
Doubtful	12	10	7	29	41.4
Unsatisfactory	2			2	100.0
Total	114	54	41	209	54.5

Summary Statistics: $\underline{C}$ = .095; γ = .176; χ^2 = 1.800; d.f. = $\underline{P}$ = .30
(Chi square computed from 3 x 2 table.)

Table 2.3

Success of Predictions against Criterion of Perseverance

Prediction	Persevered	Left	Total	% Persevered
Satisfactory	101	68	169	59.8
Doubtful	11	18	29	37.9
Unsatisfactory	2		2	100.0
Total	118	93	211	55.9

Summary Statistics: $\underline{C}$ = .130; γ = .328; χ^2 = 3.397; d.f. = 1; $\underline{P}$ = .10
(Chi square computed from 2 x 2 table.)

Table 2.4

Success of Prediction against Criterion of Ordination

Prediction	Ordained*	Left	Total	% Ordained
Satisfactory	76	56	132	57.6
Doubtful	5	14	19	26.3
Unsatisfactory	1		1	100.0
Total	85	75	160	53.1

Summary Statistics: $\underline{C}$ = .192; γ = .505; χ^2 = 5.600; d.f. = 1; $\underline{P}$ = .02
(Chi square computed from 2 x 2 table.)
  * Six were excluded because they are still in the order, although not yet ordained.

The $\underline{C}$ coefficients vary from .095 to .192. Although they are not directly comparable to Pearson's $\underline{r}$, they probably are not far below the mark; they do not indicate much relation between predictions and outcome. Some embarrassment is caused by the two men rated unsatisfactory by the psychologist. However, they do not affect the data very much because, in those cases in which they had to be grouped with the doubtful ones in order to compute χ^2, the resultant figure is not much better, unless other aspects of the data are also better. The γ coefficients are somewhat higher, although it is difficult to interpret them in terms familiar to the psychometrician. At any rate, they show some relationship between the judgment of the psychologist and the outcome, particularly in reference to the criterion of ordination to the priesthood. There is, then, some tendency for the predictions to

be verified more often than not, but there is a large margin
of error and considerable room for improvement.

Comparison with the Base Rate

Since the problem has been clearly demonstrated by Meehl
and Rosen (1955), the base rate has rather generally been
accepted as the reference point against which to evaluate
selection procedures. In the present context, one would first
determine what percentage are actually satisfactory by the
different criteria. Given this figure but no test or similar
information, he would make a prediction according to the base
rate. Thus, he would simply declare that all of the applicants
would show satisfactory mental health because 72 per cent turn
out thus, and he would be right 72 per cent of the time. If
the screening is effective, it must show improvement over this
percentage. The results of this way of analyzing the data are
given in the bottom half of Table 2.5. In determining the per

Table 2.5

Success of Predictions Compared with Base Rate

A Predictions Analyzed Separately

Prediction

	Satisfactory			Doubtful or Unsatisfactory		
Criterion	*Per Cent Correct*	*Base Rate*	*Improve- ment*	*Per Cent Correct*	*Base Rate*	*Improve- ment*
Mental Health	75.3	72.1	3.2	37.9	27.9	10.0
Adjustment	57.7	54.5	3.2	54.8	45.5	9.3
Perseverance	59.8	55.9	3.9	58.1	44.1	14.0
Ordination	57.6	53.1	4.5	70.0	46.9	23.1

B Both Predictions Combined

Criterion	*Per Cent Correct*	*Base Rate*	*Improve- ment*	γ
Mental Health	69.7	72.1	-2.4	.371
Adjustment	57.3	54.5	2.8	.176
Perseverance	59.5	55.9	3.6	.328
Ordination	59.2	53.1	6.1	.505

cent correct as to mental health and overall adjustment, the "Doubtful" and "Unsatisfactory" columns in Tables 2.1 and 2.2 were combined; thus the psychologist's judgment of "doubtful" was considered correct if the person subsequently proved either doubtful or unsatisfactory. This is reasonable, since one is hardly wrong if he has doubts about a candidate and the latter turns out to be definitely unsatisfactory. The number correct, for example, in Table 2.1 is 125 + 8 + 3 = 136, which was then divided by 195, the grand total after the exclusion of 3 who were not tested and 6 for whom there was no clear record of the psychologist's judgment. For purposes of comparison the γ coefficients are repeated.

It is clear that by this standard improvement over the base rate is very slight, 6.1 per cent at most; indeed, the record is a little worse in predicting mental health than it would have been without the tests. On the other hand, there is a difficulty about combining both favorable and unfavorable predictions in the manner described above. What is most desired in screening religious is to identify those who will likely be poor risks. For this purpose, simply to follow the base rate would accomplish nothing. Therefore, the top half of Table 2.5 was drawn up. In line with the previous reasoning, perhaps a case could be made for regarding the base rate for the unfavorable outcomes as zero because all candidates would have been passed without any stigma of doubt. The base rates given are derived from the "Total" rows in the preceding tables and provide a more realistic and conservative way of evaluating the percentages of correct judgments. There is little improvement in identifying those who will be satisfactory, roughly 3-4 per cent. However, the record is better, although still quite modest, in regard to those who are not satisfactory; here the improvement varies with the criterion from 9 to 23 per cent.

Another way of looking at the data is to see how many of the doubtful or unsatisfactory cases were actually caught. This is done in Table 2.6. The various criteria are in good agreement here: about 20 per cent were caught. This is better than nothing but far from satisfactory. The screening is clearly inadequate, at least in the long run. Furthermore, the results indicate that one has to be cautious in acting upon the psychologist's judgment when he declares a candidate doubtful or unsatisfactory. Even with the most favorable criterion, ordination to the priesthood, 30 per cent are satisfactory. This suggests that there would be considerable loss of good men if the verdict of the psychologist were followed rigidly.

Table 2.6

Identification of Those Who Were Not Satisfactory*

Criterion	Not Satisfactory	Identified	Per Cent
Mental Health	52	11	21.2
Adjustment	88	17	19.3
Perseverance	86	18	20.9
Ordination	70	14	20.0

* I.e., doubtful or unsatisfactory in mental health or adjustment; in regard to the last two criteria, failed to persevere.

Later Groups, 1956-1962

The previous discussion has concerned the first five years of the program. The sixth class, for the reasons indicated in Chapter 1, will be omitted. Since the screening procedure was somewhat changed after this, the data for subsequent years will be kept separate, and we shall now turn our attention to the classes of 1956-1962.

By way of reminder--the significant changes were the addition of a Sentence Completion Test, an interview by a psychologist for all candidates beginning with 1957, and the appointment of a different man to administer the program. From 1958 to the present, this latter psychologist has interviewed all of the men applying to one novitiate of the order, with some exceptions. For the other novitiate, the interviewing psychologist reported directly to the superior. This policy was adopted with the full realization that it might be difficult later to retrieve these reports and make use of them in research. This has proven to be true, and as a consequence the writer was unable to locate the record of 31 of the men admitted.

The follow-up has been different from that employed in the earlier group. About the end of the novitiate, information was obtained from the master of novices. This was at first done *viva voce*: the master giving a sort of brief personality description of the novice, the writer asking a few questions and taking note of the essential points. Later, it was done by correspondence. Beginning with the class of 1958 in one novitiate, the writer made use of the follow-up rating form reproduced earlier in this chapter (cf. pp. 16ff), but again *viva voce*. For the last three classes in both novitiates the rating form was simply mailed to the masters of novices, filled out at their leisure, and returned. There was some loss of detail and nuances because of this change from free description to the set form, but the data were thereby expressed in a manner which reduced the play of subjectivity in the writer's analyses. Further information was obtained later in some instances when an adjustment or study difficulty arose and the writer was consulted. For those who left after they had taken vows, the reason for leaving was ascertained whenever possible.

The method of classifying the men for mental health and overall adjustment was the same as that previously described in those cases in which the formal ratings had been obtained; in the remaining instances a certain amount of interpretation was required to adapt the detailed norms used with the earlier group. The criteria were: mental health, overall adjustment, and perseverance; only a few of these men were far enough advanced to be eligible for ordination.

The subjects were the members of seven consecutive classes who entered the novitiate. Some were excluded because of limitations in the records, inadequate basis for judging mental health or adjustment, difficulties in classifying, and so on. Approximately 40 per cent belonged to the one novitiate for which the writer does the psychological interviewing; these, and a few others whom he also saw himself, have been placed together in Group A, which totals 163. At the time of the follow-up study, the men who persevered had been in the order from four and one-half to ten and one-half years. Group B comprised the others, who numbered 247. Except for the first two classes, who were not interviewed unless the test results were doubtful, and a few instances in which the interview was waived because of practical difficulties like distance or the press of time as the entrance date drew near, they were interviewed by other psychologists. The follow-up on these men was done more than a year later, that is, from five and three-quarters to eleven and three-quarters years after entrance. This difference constituted a further reason for separating the two groups.

Results

The data with respect to the three criteria are presented in Tables 2.7--2.10. In general the results are similar to those for the earlier group. Perhaps first to note is the gradation in percentages of those who proved satisfactory (last column of Tables 2.7--2.9). As we go from those the

Table 2.7

Success of Predictions against Criterion of Mental Health

Group A

Prediction	Satis.	Doubt.	Unsat.	Total	Per Cent Satis.
Satisfactory	80	31	15	126	63.5
Doubtful	10	12	5	27	37.0
Unsatisfactory			1	1	0.0
Total*	90	45	21	156	57.7

Group B

Prediction	Satis.	Doubt.	Unsat.	Total	Per Cent Satis.
Satisfactory	128	45	8	181	70.7
Doubtful	20	11	1	32	62.5
Unsatisfactory		1		1	0.0
Total*	166	67	9	242	68.6

Both Groups

Prediction	Satis.	Doubt.	Unsat.	Total	Per Cent Satis.
Satisfactory	208	76	23	307	67.8
Doubtful	30	23	6	59	50.8
Unsatisfactory		1	1	2	0.0
Total*	256	112	30	398	64.3

* These totals include some for whom the psychologist's judgment was no longer on record.

Table 2.8

Success of Predictions against Criterion of Overall Adjustme

Group A

Prediction	Satis.	Doubt.	Unsat.	Total	Per Cent Satis.
Satisfactory	55	21	49	125	44.0
Doubtful	8	10	17	35	22.9
Unsatisfactory			1	1	0.0
Total*	63	32	68	163	38.7

Group B

Prediction	Satis.	Doubt.	Unsat.	Total	Per Cent Satis.
Satisfactory	93	59	30	182	51.1
Doubtful	12	15	7	34	35.3
Unsatisfactory		1		1	0.0
Total*	120	84	42	246	48.8

Both Groups

Prediction	Satis.	Doubt.	Unsat.	Total	Per Cent Satis.
Satisfactory	148	80	79	307	48.2
Doubtful	20	25	24	69	29.0
Unsatisfactory		1	1	2	0.0
Total*	183	116	110	409	44.7

* These totals include some for whom the psychologist's judgment was no longer on record.

Table 2.9

Success of Predictions against Criterion of Perseverance

Group A

Prediction	Persevered	Left	Total	Per Cent Persevered
Satisfactory	57	66	123	46.3
Doubtful	11	26	37	29.7
Unsatisfactory		1	1	0.0
Total*	69	94	163	42.3

Group B

Prediction	Persevered	Left	Total	Per Cent Persevered
Satisfactory	92	91	183	50.3
Doubtful	12	22	34	35.3
Unsatisfactory		1	1	0.0
Total*	115	132	247	46.6

Both Groups

Prediction	Persevered	Left	Total	Per Cent Persevered
Satisfactory	149	157	306	48.7
Doubtful	23	48	71	32.4
Unsatisfactory		2	2	0.0
Total*	184	226	410	44.9

* These totals include some for whom the psychologist's judgment was no longer on record.

Table 2.10

Success of Predictions in Terms of $\underline{C}$, γ, and χ^2

Groups Separately

| | Group A | | | | Group B | | | |
Criterion	$\underline{C}$	γ	χ^2	$\underline{P}$	$\underline{C}$	γ	χ^2	$\underline{P}$
Mental Health	.217	.441	7.278	.01*	.079	.198	1.338	.3
Adjustment	.192	.297	5.965	.10	.126	.245	3.429	.2
Perseverance	.150	.362	3.560	.10*	.117	.322	3.010	.1

Both Groups Combined

Criterion	$\underline{C}$	γ	χ^2	$\underline{P}$
Mental Health	.145	.334	7.690	.05
Adjustment	.158	.293	9.387	.01
Perseverance	.136	.350	7.023	.01*

* Chi square computed from 2 x 2 table; otherwise from 3 x 2.

psychologist originally declared satisfactory down to those he thought unsatisfactory, we find a decrease in the percentages of satisfactory outcome. This trend is clearest according to the perseverance criterion, regardless of the group. In Group A it is more pronounced according to all three criteria. The degree of association between prediction and outcome can best be evaluated statistically by the figures in Table 2.10. For Group B, the $\underline{C}$ and γ coefficients are about the same as for the earlier investigation, while for Group A they are a little better: $\underline{C}$ ranges from .150 to .217 as against .095 to .130 for the earlier study and .079 to .126 for Group B; γ runs from .297 to .441 as against .176 to .371 and .198 to .322 respectively. By the Chi-square test, none of these coefficients are statistically significant except the two for the criterion of mental health in Group A. This is not very encouraging. However, when both of the current subgroups are combined, both coefficients are significant for all three criteria and they are pretty much the same as for Group A. On the other hand, they do not suggest more than an extremely modest degree of association, and the combination of the subgroups is somewhat risky.

It would appear on the face of it, that better results have been obtained when the same psychologist handles both the tests and the interview (Group A). This is a possibility, but no statistical test was applied to differences between the two sets of results, partly because of difficulty finding the appropriate statistic but mostly because it appears unlikely that the differences would be significant. As far as the C and γ coefficients are concerned, they are not themselves statistically significant for the most part. As far as the percentages in Tables 2.7--2.9 go, the comparatively small number of cases for each subcategory would almost certainly render them unreliable.

A further discussion of the γ coefficients is in order, but let us restrict ourselves to those that proved significant: .441 for the mental-health criterion in Group A, and .334, .293, and .350 for the three criteria when both groups are combined. While these are not impressive, they are much like the correlation coefficients often obtained in the use of aptitude tests, and would be considered as pointing to the validity of the tests. In a more exact evaluation, one would square the correlation and conclude that the square indicates the proportion of variance in the criterion measure that is in some way accounted for by the test variance. For the highest value we have here, that would be $.441^2$, which is .194 or roughly 20 per cent. But γ is not a correlation; it concerns more directly the success of predictions. Using the same value by way of example, let us go back to some of the figures that may be obtained in the course of the computation. (They are not given in Table 2.10.) If we take two men who have been examined by the psychologist and find that one is better than the other, then there is a 72 per cent chance that he will be better in the criterion classification and a 28 per cent chance that he will be worse; the chance, thus, of being right in the initial evaluation exceeds the chance of the direct opposite by 44 per cent. Note the studious avoidance of the word *wrong*: such a prediction could be wrong because the two were rated the same according to the criterion (tied, in other words) or because their relative position turned out to be exactly opposite to that predicted. This is a limitation of this statistic: it ignores ties, and on either variable; hence, it would seem to give an inflated value, since it really counts only the greater errors. Yet we can at least say that it shows a considerably greater chance of being right than of making a gross error.

A comparison of the predictions with the base rate is given in Table 2.11. In this case the two subgroups are combined. When those originally judged satisfactory are

31

Table 2.11

Success of Predictions Compared with Base Rate

A Predictions Analyzed Separately

Prediction

	Satisfactory			Doubtful or Unsatisfact		
Criterion	*Per Cent Correct*	*Base Rate*	*Improve-ment*	*Per Cent Correct*	*Base Rate*	*Improve-ment*
Mental Health	67.8	64.3	3.5	50.8	35.7	15.1
Adjustment	48.2	44.7	3.5	71.8	55.3	16.5
Perseverance	48.7	44.9	3.8	68.5	55.1	13.4

B Both Predictions Combined

Criterion	*Per Cent Correct*	*Base Rate*	*Improve-ment*	γ
Mental Health	64.9	64.3	.6	.334
Adjustment	52.6	44.7	7.9	.293
Perseverance	52.5	44.9	7.6	.350

kept separate from those judged doubtful or unsatisfactory
and evaluated against the corresponding base rate, the record is fundamentally the same as for the earlier group,
although generally just a little better. As before, the
overall percentages of correct judgments do not improve
very much over the base rate. We see also the same relation
between the favorable and unfavorable judgments: the former
show only a slight improvement, even though the base rate
is in the neighborhood of 50 per cent, which would give the
best chance of improvement. The psychologists were more successful in their unfavorable predictions. And the improvement in this group is more consistent from criterion to
criterion than in the earlier group; the figures stay rather close to 15 per cent. The actual percentages of correct
predictions tell us that the psychologists were right in
about two-thirds of the judgments regarding mental health,
and in about half of the cases if overall adjustment or
perseverance is taken as the criterion. For the favorable
judgments considered separately, the story is the same.
For the unfavorable judgments, there is greater variability
from criterion to criterion: for mental health it is only
51 per cent; for adjustment and perseverance, approximate-

ly 70 per cent. Regardless of the way the data are examined, it appears that the record is not very flattering.

So far the point of approach has been the accuracy of the psychologists' judgments. Let us now reverse the viewpoint and consider the cases which *de facto* proved doubtful or unsatisfactory and determine how many of these were identified correctly in advance. Table 2.12 shows that at best only 29 per cent of these were detected in the screening procedure and that on the average the figure would come to about 25 per cent. Results are somewhat better with Group A than with Group B, again suggesting that it is better to have the same man handle both tests and interview; but, of course, no evidence has been presented that the differences are significant, for the reasons indicated a few pages before this. There is also an improvement over the 19 to 21 per cent obtained in the earlier study, but it is far from the great improvement expected when the decision was reached to interview everyone, regardless of the test results. (The observant reader will recall that, with the first class

Table 2.12

Identification of Those Who Were Not Satisfactory*

Group A

Criterion	Not Satisfactory	Identified	Per Cent
Mental Health	64	18	28.1
Adjustment	98	28	28.6
Perseverance	93	27	29.0

Group B

Mental Health	66	13	18.2
Adjustment	112	23	20.5
Perseverance	114	23	20.2

Both Groups

Mental Health	130	31	23.8
Adjustment	210	51	24.3
Perseverance	207	50	24.2

* I.e., doubtful or unsatisfactory in mental health or adjustment; left, in regard to the perseverance criterion.

under study here, only some were interviewed; he may wish
to object to the inclusion of these cases with the rest.
However, separate tabulations, which are not reproduced
here, show that their exclusion would not influence the
results appreciably.) But the effectiveness of the interview as against the tests alone will be considered more
thoroughly later in this chapter.

Effect of Testing on Rate of Perseverance

A question occasionally asked is whether perseverance
has been improved since the inception of the psychological
testing. Table 2.13 shows that the answer must be no and
that, on the contrary, it is a bit worse. However, these
are the brute facts; their meaning is not entirely clear.
The 1945-1949 years are taken as a reference group; but
they are not completely typical, since they saw the influx
of a sizeable proportion of men who had been in the Armed
Forces, were more mature and probably better motivated than
the younger men. There is a general trend down, which would
most likely be even more evident if the figure for 1960-
1964 were corrected a few years from now.

Table 2.13

Rates of Perseverance Before and After
    Inception of the Screening Program (1950)

Years	*Entered*	*Persevered*
1945-1949	196	58.7%
1950-1954	211	55.9
1955-1959	289	50.2
1960-1964	309	54.0

In as far as the above question is meant as a challenge
to the value of the screening program, a better approach
is to consider the percentages of perseverance among those
originally rated satisfactory. These are contained in Tables
2.3 and 2.9, as well as 2.5 and 2.11; they are 59.8 per
cent (against a base rate of 55.9) and 48.7 per cent (against
a base rate of 44.9). These figures manifest a very small
improvement. But it must be remembered that the base rates
are taken from the screened groups and are raised somewhat
by the inclusion of the satisfactory men. (The same point
can also be made in reference to the discussion of Tables
2.5 and 2.9 earlier in this chapter.)

Various specific points have been made in the previous discussion. It is time now to draw together the principal conclusions that emerge. To do so, it will be necessary to express figures approximately; and ranges will have to be given in order to avoid constant reference to the various criteria.

1   Although the data in their rawest form seem to suggest that mental health is predicted better than overall adjustment, perseverance, or reaching ordination, closer analysis, particularly from the standpoint of improvement over the base rate, does not support this conclusion. The various criteria give about the same results, with exceptions that could easily be due to chance.

2   The overall percentage of correct judgments made by the psychologist varies with the criterion and the group: 60-70 for the earlier classes and 50-65 for the later. Improvement over the base rate runs from -2 to +8 per cent.

3   However, the psychologist's judgment of "satisfactory" is right in 60-75 and 50-70 per cent of the cases in the two groups respectively. Improvement over the base rate is 3-4 per cent. When the judgment is "doubtful" or "unsatisfactory," the percentages correct are 40-70 and 50-70, for an improvement of 10-25. Hence, the unfavorable predictions are more successful than the favorable.

4   On the other hand, of those who do turn out to be less than satisfactory, only 20-30 per cent are actually caught by the screening; the "screen" is very coarse.

5   Finally, results with the program are better than without it, but how much better they are depends on the criterion, what exactly is taken as the goal, and from what aspect the data are approached. The writer feels that the objective is to identify the unsuited, and in this regard the improvement achieved is 10-25 or 20-30 per cent according to the figures just given in #3 and #4. This is disappointing.

A Further Assessment of Accuracy

In the course of the follow-up of the men at the end of the novitiate, one year the master of novices spontaneously changed his method of reporting: for about half of the class he began his descriptions by stating, "You were right on this one," "You were wrong," or some equivalent expression. And he did the same with almost all of the men in the following year. This was a windfall for the writer, since it provided a rather simple means of determining the accuracy of the predictions, at least in the estimation of the novices' director.

There were, of course, difficulties. For one thing, he would sometimes add, "Except," and then go on to list things that did not seem to support the original statement regarding correctness. Secondly, he made these evaluations with the original report before him, and it is a moot question to what extent suggestion may have influenced his judgment. But on the other hand, there were a number of cases in which he disagreed quite bluntly; for example, he once stated, "Just take the opposite of what you said, and you will be right." A third difficulty was the dependence on the opinion of one man—but this has been discussed previously.

There were 50 cases involved. The original reports were classified on the basis of this information as (1) correct, (2) mostly correct, and (3) wrong or only partially correct. The writer did not always accept at face value the statement that his report had been correct. When further comments indicated that there might be some doubt about the matter, he classified the prediction as mostly correct or partly correct; in these instances, the judgment of the writer may well have been biased in his own favor; however, he was acutely aware of the problem and tended to be more rather than less severe. As previously, it was the question of confidentiality that deterred him from seeking an independent judgment.

The results are presented in Table 2.14. By this criterion the accuracy of the reports comes out much better than by the others which have been used. The master of novices considered 64 per cent simply correct. With the addition of the cases which were mostly correct, the percentage is 80. This is a rather respectable figure. If there is some bias in adding these intervening cases, it is probably balanced by placing the partially correct with the wrong (3 of the 10).

Table 2.14

Classification of Psychologist's Reports
    According to Judgment of the Master of Novices

	Number	*Percentage*
Correct	32	64.0
Mostly Correct	8	16.0
Partially Correct or Wrong	10	20.0

What is the import of this more favorable evidence for the value of the psychological assessment, and why the difference? Possibly the psychologist is generally correct in describing the candidate's personality but frequently makes mistakes in the inferential step from description to prediction. The judgment of satisfactory, doubtful, or unsatisfactory is a conclusion, and the personality description amounts to the premises of the conclusion. Perhaps it is between these two that the error creeps in. Of course, if a rigorous critic wishes to discount these favorable results on the score of suggestion, there is no way of gainsaying him. A final observation is in order: this is essentially the reaction that the screening program has received from the "consumers," the superiors and particularly the masters of novices—and that despite two rather unfavorable reports given them by the writer. At least the present data serve to document the reaction of one of them.

Tests Versus Interview

In the 1962 study the hope was expressed that the assessment process would be improved if all the applicants were interviewed by a psychologist. Hence, after the accumulation of sufficient data, a check was made of this assumption.

The novices who entered in 1957-1962 were selected for study. These formed two groups: those interviewed by the author (Group A) and those examined by other psychologists (Group B). There were 138 in the first group and 188 in the second. It will be recalled that the 1957 entrants were not all interviewed by the author, although he nevertheless made the final judgment about their fitness. After that, all in the one novitiate were seen by him; in the other, the psychologist who did the interviewing reported directly to the superior. There were some exceptions to this pattern, but they were quite rare. In order to be able later to distinguish between the results of the tests and those of the follow-up interview, a preliminary judgment was made before the interview even in those cases handled entirely by the author.

There are some qualifications which need to be specified in order to avoid giving the impression that the two phases of the process were entirely distinct. First, in the earlier years further tests were often used in doubtful cases, and always the other psychologist was free to use more tests if he saw fit. Hence, when reference is made to the interview, this must be understood as including these tests. Second, when reference is made to the results of the tests, this means the two routinely used and all the other information derived from the paper work. These last sources, naturally, would often throw considerable light on the findings and alter the interpretation perhaps radically. Third, the interview is not at all independent of the preceding tests or the judgment based on their interpretation. The author could not ignore the impression of the candidate he had already formed. The other psychologists had before them a formal report made by the author, had generally been requested to check certain points, and must certainly have been influenced to some extent. (On the other hand, there is a possibility that sometimes there might have been a sort of negative suggestion, particularly as the years went by and the author leaned more and more to the strategy of declaring a candidate "doubtful" if there was anything of even moderate importance that needed to be cleared up.) Hence, the comparison is not properly between tests and the interview alone, but between tests (or paper material) and the whole process capped by the interview.

As in the studies previously reported in this chapter, the criteria are: mental health, overall adjustment, and perseverance. The source of information and the scheme of classification were the same as previously indicated for the 1956–1962 group, of which these ones are, of course, a part.

In Table 2.15, which lists the basic data, the heading of the first column may be a little confusing. For the sake of brevity, the term "original judgment" is used merely in the sense of "preceding admission," although the adjective may in itself suggest the tentative judgment based on the tests. The totals indicated in the table give us the actual percentages of subjects in this group who met the various criteria; they are the base rates for their respective categories in this and the following two tables.

A number of conclusions are suggested by the first table, but we shall concentrate on the main question in hand. It is clear that the interview does not add any striking precision to the procedure, to say the least. Generally the interview turns out a little better than the tests alone in regard to the unfavorable judgments, but at the expense of the favorable judgments; in either case the difference is trivial.

Table 2.15

Judgment Based on Tests versus Judgment after Interview,
    According to Three Criteria

Group A

			Outcome	
Criterion	*Source of Information*	*Original Judgment*	*Satis.*	*D. or U.*
Mental Health	Tests	Satisfactory	74.0%	26.0%
		Doubt. or Unsat.	37.1	62.9
	Interview	Satisfactory	71.8	28.2
		Doubt. or Unsat.	35.7	64.3
		Total*	64.1	35.9
Adjustment	Tests	Satisfactory	57.6	42.4
		Doubt. or Unsat.	28.2	71.8
	Interview	Satisfactory	56.6	43.4
		Doubt. or Unsat.	25.0	75.0
		Total*	49.3	50.7
Perseverance**	Tests	Satisfactory	51.5	48.5
		Doubt. or Unsat.	28.2	71.8
	Interview	Satisfactory	49.1	50.9
		Doubt. or Unsat.	31.2	68.8
		Total*	44.9	55.1

Group B

Mental Health	Tests	Satisfactory	75.7	24.3
		Doubt. or Unsat.	61.0	39.0
	Interview	Satisfactory	71.2	28.8
		Doubt. or Unsat.	61.3	38.7
		Total*	69.6	30.4
Adjustment	Tests	Satisfactory	56.6	43.4
		Doubt. or Unsat.	40.2	59.8
	Interview	Satisfactory	52.9	47.1
		Doubt. or Unsat.	33.3	66.7
		Total*	49.5	50.5
Perseverance**	Tests	Satisfactory	51.9	48.1
		Doubt. or Unsat.	45.1	54.9
	Interview	Satisfactory	52.3	47.7
		Doubt. or Unsat.	33.3	66.7
		Total*	48.9	51.1

    * These percentages will be used as base rates in sub-
sequent analyses.
    ** As to perseverance, "Satisfactory Outcome" means per-
severance, "Doubtful or Unsatisfactory," failure to persevere.

Because it is difficult from these data to get a clear picture of the improvement or lack of it, Table 2.16 has been prepared. In this table the percentages of judgments that proved correct, whether initially favorable or unfavorable, are given. The base rate is subtracted from these, to give a measure of improvement. As can be seen, the interview comes out a little worse than the tests in Group A, and, on balance, a little better in Group B. It is surely safe to say that the data again fail to show any real advantage for the interview.

Table 2.16

Predictive Success of Tests and Interview in Terms of Percentage Correct

	Tests			Interview	
Criterion	Base Rate	Cor-rect	Improve-ment	Cor-rect	Improve-ment
Group A					
Mental Health	64.1	71.0	6.9	70.2	6.1
Adjustment	49.3	61.6	12.3	60.9	11.6
Perseverance	44.9	57.2	12.3	53.6	8.7
Group B					
Mental Health	69.6	60.3	-9.3	65.8	-3.8
Adjustment	49.5	58.0	8.5	55.3	5.8
Perseverance	48.9	53.2	4.3	54.8	5.9

Another consideration, closer in fact to the primary purpose of the screening, is the identification of problem cases, that is, those who do not prove satisfactory. Here again the interview proves of dubious value. In Group A it does a little better than the tests in identifying those who turn out satisfactory, and in Group B its superiority is rather pronounced. But it does appreciably worse in catching those who are not satisfactory, particularly for Group B, in which the tests do about twice as well. The data are shown in Table 2.17.

Table 2.17

Previous Data from Standpoint of Identifying Problem Cases

| | | Identified by: | |
	Actual	Tests	Interview
Group A			
Mental Health			
Satisfactory	64.1%	84.5%	88.1%
Doubt. or Unsat.	35.9	46.8	38.3
Adjustment			
Satisfactory	49.3	83.8	88.2
Doubt. or Unsat.	50.7	40.0	34.3
Perseverance			
Persevered	44.9	82.3	83.9
Left	55.1	36.8	28.9
Group B			
Mental Health			
Satisfactory	69.6	63.3	85.2
Doubt. or Unsat.	30.4	53.6	21.4
Adjustment			
Satisfactory	49.5	64.5	88.2
Doubt. or Unsat.	50.5	51.6	23.2
Perseverance			
Persevered	48.9	59.8	88.0
Left	51.1	46.9	22.9

An interesting sidelight is the progression of percentages correct with the various criteria. For this point let
us return to Table 2.16, take the data for the interview,
round to whole numbers, and place the percentages for Groups
A and B adjacent to one another. The percentages of correct
judgments are: 54-55 for the perseverance criterion, 55-61
for adjustment, and 66-70 for mental health. The roughest,
least precise, and least intended in the first place is the
criterion of perseverance; adjustment gets closer to the
mark; while mental health is the criterion most directly
related to the original purpose of the screening and the
point of major emphasis in the psychologists' reports. What
is to be concluded? Apparently this: As the criterion becomes
more and more appropriate, the degree of accuracy increases.
But what of the 80 per cent correct when the judgment of the
master of novices was the criterion (cf. the preceding sec-

tion of this chapter)? The increase may simply reflect a
tendency to look benignly on the psychologist's work--a real
and, in a sense, frightening phenomenon in the experience
of the writer. However, it may represent a sort of refinement of the criterion: The master of novices, except in a
few cases, had the personality descriptions before him and
was judging the extent to which these fit the novices. To
this extent his judgment was a more exacting criterion than
the others.

Table 2.18 presents the C and γ coefficients for the
same data. As far as Group A is concerned, these figures
agree with the preceding in showing the tests slightly superior to the interview, but the result is reversed with
Group B. In the latter case the coefficients generally run
somewhat lower and are less significant statistically than
in the first group. By way of conclusion, one may safely
say that there is no evidence here of any real advantage
of one method of screening over the other.

Table 2.18

Predictive Success of Tests and Interview in Terms of
   C and γ

Criterion	Tests			Interview		
	C	γ	P	C	γ	P
Group A						
Mental Health	.340	.581	.001	.309	.570	.001
Adjustment	.265	.456	.01	.267	.478	.01
Perseverance	.211	.460	.02	.156	.359	.10
Group B						
Mental Health	.157	.331	.05	.081	.220	.30
Adjustment	.162	.319	.05	.149	.384	.05
Perseverance	.067	.135	.50	.144	.373	.05

In the course of making the various tabulations of the
data, an impression was formed that the main locus of error
was in the changes from the "doubtful" and "unsatisfactory"
to the "satisfactory" judgments. Consequently a check was
made, with perseverance as the criterion. There were 10
such changes in Group A and 42 in Group B, for a total of

52. The perseverance rate of these 52 was 65.4 per cent,
which is quite good in comparison with the base rate of
45.1 per cent for the combined groups. Clearly this type of
opinion-change is not the major source of error. As to the
reverse shift, from "satisfactory" to "doubtful" or "unsatisfactory," there were 33 cases and only 7 (21.2 per
cent) persevered. Hence, both sorts of change actually made
for greater accuracy. In fact, these latter figures, in
contrast with those seen previously in this section, suggest that the interview does make a valuable contribution
after all.

A similar point which emerged from this analysis was
the following: There were 49 instances in which both tests
and interview were unfavorable. (That is, both showings
were "doubtful," both "unsatisfactory," or one "doubtful"
and the other "unsatisfactory.") The perseverance rate for
these men was 20.4 per cent, as of the time of writing.
This suggests that, when both tests and interview agree that
a candidate is at best of doubtful promise, the chances of
perseverance are very poor.

It will be observed that the numbers of cases involved
in the data presented in the last two paragraphs are small.
This, of course, makes for limited reliability of these
figures. But, aside from this, it serves to explain why we
suddenly find favorable evidence for the interview and, on
the other hand, to call attention to an important limitation.
In the three comparisons, there were 52, 33, and 49 cases,
representing 15.9, 10.1, and 14.9 per cent of the total
(328 for Groups A and B combined). Hence, the improvement
indicated pertains to only a small proportion of the whole
group. This improvement has relatively little effect on
statistics involving the whole group, as in Tables 2.15 to
2.18; and this is why we obtain disappointing results with
the grosser analysis and encouraging results with the finer.
As to the limitation referred to above, it seems that the
interview works very well when it works, but it doesn't
work often enough: that is, when it modifies the judgment
of the candidate's fitness it tends strongly to be correct,
and when it confirms an unfavorable judgment it is also generally correct. But it does not do so well when it passes
those already passed by the tests; in other words, it does
not succeed in identifying enough of the problem cases, as
was previous indicated in the discussion of Table 2.17.

Conclusions

Most of the statistics presented in this chapter suggest
that the interview does not add to the general accuracy of

the screening, if it does not actually cause further error. But treating the data *en bloc*, as in Tables 2.15 to 2.18, appears to obscure some real improvement. When attention is paid to the precise nature of the changes in judgments about candidates resulting from the interview, accuracy is, after all, increased. A number of the doubtful candidates come out as satisfactory, and correctly so. A number of those who had first been passed as satisfactory are correctly identified as doubtful at best. Where the interview seems to fall down is that it still passes too many.

There are, of course, some additional considerations in favor of interviewing all candidates. In the first place, it must be remembered that there has been no follow-up of the candidates who were rejected. The majority of these had been classed as doubtful or unsatisfactory according to tests, interview, or both. On occasion, the lack of emotional stability had been so clear that there was little doubt of the matter. These cases, however, cannot be included in the statistics because there was no external confirmation independent of the psychologist's judgment. And there were always some borderline cases in which one would hesitate as to the degree of clarity.

Another consideration in favor of the interview is this: Often the recommendation was made that a candidate be admitted "as a risk" because of compensating qualities. More often still, the report called attention to possible trouble areas to be watched and met with special counseling. Usually such decisions or recommendations could not be made with any confidence before the interview. To distinguish these cases from the rest and classify them separately would be fairly awkward and would pose the constant problem of small subgroups and the consequent unreliability of any statistics derived therefrom. This difficulty about special cases, it may be added, affects the satisfactory group as well as the doubtful.

Again, there was a practical matter: one of morale. When the policy had been to interview only those who were doubtful on the basis of the tests, there were some unpleasant reactions from the people involved. Some candidates were disturbed because they were called in while others were immediately passed, and angry parents entered the picture. Some felt they "had flunked the psychological tests" and were either resentful or worried. Such reactions can make evaluation difficult. The solution of not interviewing even doubtful cases would hardly be defensible clinically, nor would it accord with the data on those cases in which a change was made from an unfavorable to a favorable decision on the basis of the interview. Hence, practical considerations would dictate continuing the present procedure.

Furthermore, the writer's experience, which he cannot support by marshalling statistics because of the small number of cases entailed and the lack of adequate follow-up evidence, indicates that it has value in preventing the admission of some very poor risks who would otherwise have slipped through.

In final conclusion, it may be said that the interview does not increase the accuracy of prediction *overall*. But it does correct the test results in an appreciable number of cases, although it misses a larger proportion of poor risks than one should like.

Bad Misses versus Hits

One of the most distressing features of the screening program to date has been the failure to catch some applicants who later became quite disturbed. These men cause considerable trouble to the religious superiors and prompt serious doubts about the adequacy of the screening program. In the 1962 study the number of such cases was determined for the first four classes which had been screened. Similarly, the records of those who had not been accepted were searched for cases in which the psychologist had successfully detected the presence or threat of pathology. Those not detected were called "clear misses"; those detected, "clear hits." The criterion for determining the misses was the development of mental illness in religious life. For the hits, all but one of whom had been refused admission, the criterion was subsequent behavior that clearly indicated instability or confirmation of the psychologist's opinion by a psychiatrist. Unless a candidate actually enters the novitiate, it is rather difficult to obtain further information about him; hence, some data on this side of the ledger are lost--probably to the detriment of the psychologist's success record.

The results showed 9 clear misses and 6 clear hits for a period of four years, so that the yearly average was a bit more than 2 misses and between 1 and 2 hits. This is not an impressive achievement, to say the least. On the other hand, when a major superior was asked whether this small return was worth all the man-hours required by the screening, he replied unhesitatingly that it was.

The data for the fifth and sixth classes could not be used because the information contained in the files was not adequate. For subsequent years it is possible to continue this sort of analysis: hence, this was done for the later classes. However, besides mental illness, other conditions indicative of unfitness were included in the criteria.

First, the records were examined in regard to mental illness. It was necessary to spell out the guidelines in some detail in order to maintain consistency and make for objectivity. A person was classed as unfit from the mental health standpoint if he:

(1) developed a mental illness *after* he had taken the tests, and this illness was verified by the diagnosis of a psychiatrist or another psychologist, or was completely obvious in his behavior; or

(2) showed a very marked disturbance, (a) involving psychiatric consultation and treatment, with the final advice to leave the order, or (b) requiring long psychiatric treatment, or (c) requiring treatment by a psychologist which turned out unsuccessful, or (d) needing the use of tranquilizers for a long period. The very marked disturbances included severe anxiety and real phobias. Psychosomatic illness was not counted unless it led to psychiatric treatment; nor were immaturity and marked emotionality counted. It will be noted that the mental illness, and indeed the other disturbances, were to have occurred after the tests had been given. This specification was made in order to exclude the cases in which the original judgment of unfitness was determined or strongly influenced by a history of previous mental illness. Perhaps this is unfair to the psychologist, but it avoids contaminating the criterion by including evidence used in the prediction itself. However, there were occasional cases in which there had been some previous indications of mental illness, the candidate was admitted as a risk, and later showed either mental illness or marked disturbance; for example, one man had experienced what might have been a neurotic depressive reaction, had shown good recovery from this, but later developed persistent emotional upheaval with some depressive features.

The second criterion was added because it was felt that restricting one's attention to mental illness was losing some of the data which actually bear on the success of the screening. It did not seem accurate, for instance, to ignore cases in which the psychologist, although he had no worries about any threat of serious mental illness, nevertheless thought that the candidate might develop psychosomatic ills, might cause trouble behaviorally, or did not have a good chance of persevering. Consequently the norms were:

(1) psychosomatic illness involving psychological treatment; or

(2) blackouts; or

(3) the need of some psychological treatment beyond just one or two interviews; or

(4) indecision, shown by withdrawal of application without good reason, or which persisted for a long time in the novitiate and right up to the taking of vows or until the decision to leave was finally made; or

(5) instability of purpose, that is, coming to the novitiate with no intention of staying, wanting to leave almost at once upon arrival, leaving in the first week or two (except when the reason was discovery of a canonical impediment or some similar fact which made leaving the only possible course of action); or

(6) confusion as to faith or goals; or

(7) behavior such that dismissal or voluntary separation was called for, or general "playboy" behavior.

Some of these specifications perhaps call for further elucidation. Blackouts were occasionally reported under stress or when reading or speaking before a group; these are included because they are probably psychosomatic in these circumstances. Psychological treatment, that is, by a psychologist and not a psychiatrist, posed a problem, since there were some instances in which superiors simply wanted professional advice, others in which the novice had encountered some problem and wanted an opinion about its seriousness or needed a little reassurance. In these cases, one could hardly speak of treatment; hence these cases were not counted. The question of indecision also caused some trouble in classification. It is not at all unusual for the novice to have moments in which he questions the wisdom of his choice; in fact, he can quite normally have his doubts for some time. If he works out of these and comes to a firm decision, he can hardly be taxed with unfitness. On the other hand, if the indecision persists so that finally he is told to leave or comes to see that this is the only solution, he is not fit for a life under vows, even though he may not be mentally unsound. And, strangely enough, there has been an occasional instance in which a man was indecisive up to almost the moment of taking vows; no one who has any knowledge of the religious life would consider this condition benign. One may quarrel with the inclusion of cases in which the novice left within the first two weeks. There are two lines of reasoning here. First, if the novice then found that the religious life was different from what he thought, he could not have made an informed, rational decision in the first place, he seems to have acted immaturely. Second, if he knew what he was about and changed his mind so readily, he had not made a firm decision. The psychologist had often remarked in his report or in his notes that he saw nothing wrong with the man from the standpoint of mental health but simply doubted the firmness of his decision or the likelihood of perseverance. These cases, then, ought to be included if there is to be any balanced reckoning of his success at prediction. By "confusion as to faith and goals" is meant a very real confusion, a thoroughly mixed up condition, not merely some doubts or intelligent questioning. As to the "playboy" activity, this does not mean any gross moral offenses, but merely a rather complete failure to realize that the religious life is a serious undertaking and requires buckling down to meet its demands. As in the case of indecision, the psychologist had often predicted that the candidate would have trouble with the demands of obedience. In this connection, it may be noted that there were some instances in which behavior antecedent to the tests verged on the sociopathic, left little doubt that the candidate was unfit, and constituted the main reason for rejection; but such cases were not counted for the same reason as that given above in reference to previous mental illness.

The original predictions were expressed for the most part in the manner described in Chapter 1, that is, the applicant was declared satisfactory, doubtful, or unsatisfactory from the standpoint of personality. As the years went on and follow-up data were accumulated, the writer tended more and more to add other qualifications to his report, particularly in regard to the definiteness of the candidate's decision and his likelihood of perseverance. On occasion, the statement regarding perseverance was confined to his notes, not included in the report, so as to avoid the risk of prejudicing the master of novices. Another frequent qualification was the suspicion of a tendency to psychosomatic illness.

Most of those declared doubtful were admitted. When a man is classified as caught by the screening, this means that the psychologist had at least doubted his suitability, even though he may have made the positive recommendation of admission as a risk. There is not always a perfect correspondence between the reasons given for the doubt and the precise trouble that arose later; thus, for example, while the doubt may have concerned the possibility of a schizoid personality, the trouble that eventuated may have been anxiety. If the classification is "missed," this means that the psychologist did not predict any of the characteristics given among the criterion guidelines detailed above.

The basis of the predictions is not always as cleancut as one might wish for research purposes. It will be recalled that the first class was not interviewed except when the tests left some doubt about fitness. But the major difficulty was posed by candidates who had been marked "doubtful" or "unsatisfactory" but had not been interviewed because they withdrew their application in the meantime. Including these cases may introduce some error. For example, a number of these unfavorable judgments might have been reversed after interview. The reason for tolerating this source of error is simply to avoid discarding, right and left, data that really are significant for evaluating the screening program.

The results are presented in Table 2.19. A separate count was made for the two criteria: mental health and other undesirable conditions, and finally for the two combined. The total number examined, the yearly average, and the percentages of the total are given in a footnote.

Table 2.19

Undesirable Candidates Caught and Missed by the
     Screening Program

| | Mental Illness | | Other Conditions | | Both Conditions | |
	No.	Per Year	No.	Per Year	No.	Per Year
Caught	9	1.3	34	4.9	43	6.1
Missed	17	2.4	57	8.1	74	10.6
Total	26	3.7	91	13.0	117	16.7

Note--Number examined: 520; mean per year: 74.3. The undesirables regarding mental illness, other conditions, and both together constitute the following percentages of the total respectively: 5.0, 17.5, and 22.5.

From the figures pertaining to mental health, it can be seen that the record is similar to that obtained with the earlier classes in the 1962 study: about 1 hit annually and 2 misses. The number caught would be a little better if one could get clear information from an independent source regarding some rejected candidates who had been considered very obviously disturbed or otherwise unfit. But the writer could not use his own judgment as both predictor and criterion, although he has little doubt that he was right about these men. Be this as it may, the bothersome fact is that the screening program is consistently missing some bad cases.

For the conditions other than mental health, about 5 are caught annually and 8 are missed. (Incidentally, if we tabulate those only whose tests and interview are handled by the same psychologist, these figures are almost exactly reversed: 9 caught and 6 missed.) These results are a bit more favorable, but they still leave one with the conclusion that too many are missed. On the other hand, some of these conditions, for example, confusion as to faith or goals, go somewhat beyond the scope of the tests and are hard to detect in anything less than extended counseling sessions. But again, we are led to the same conclusion: the screening does some good, but it falls short of the hopes many have had for it.

Notes

1 The numbers were not on the form; they were later used as code numbers for recording and classifying.

2 In bringing the results up to date, this stricture was changed, as will be explained later.

3 For Cramér's $\underline{C}$, cf. Kendall and Stuart, 1961, p. 557. This is not the same as the coefficient of mean square contingency, which is also called $\underline{C}$ or $\underline{CC}$. It is a method of using χ^2 to obtain an index of association which varies between 0 and 1 and can actually reach 1 even with few categories; χ^2 also serves to provide an estimate of its statistical significance. With a 2 x 2 table, $\underline{C}$ gives the same numerical results as ϕ.

For γ, cf. Goodman and Kruskal, 1954, pp. 747–54. This statistic is designed for classes which are ordered along some dimension. It expresses the probability that two persons, chosen at random from the sample, will maintain the same relative order on the criterion variable as on the predictor. Thus the figure of .371 in Table 2.1 means that there is a 37.1 per cent better chance that any two such subjects will be found in the same order than in a reverse order. The supposition, however, is that they will not be tied.

4 There were two reasons for this: first, to reduce by a week or two the delay in deciding on the application; second, because the interviewer would be in a better position to make the final decision regarding psychological fitness and the psychologist in general charge would in practice have to accede to his opinion rather than rely on the test results and a necessarily short summary of the interview.

References

Goodman, Leo A. and William H. Kruskal. Measures of association for cross classifications. *J. Amer. Stat. Assoc.*, 1954, 49, 732-64.

Kendall, Maurice G. and Alan Stuart. *The Advanced Theory of Statistics*. Vol. 2: *Inference and Relationship*. London: Charles Griffin; and New York: Hafner, 1961.

Meehl, Paul E. and Albert Rosen. Antecedent probability and the efficiency of psychometric signs, patterns, or cutting scores. *Psychol. Bull.*, 1955, 52, 194-216.

Weisgerber, Charles A., S.J. Survey of a psychological screening program in a clerical order. In Magda B. Arnold, *et al. Screening Candidates for the Priesthood and Religious Life*. Chicago: Loyola University Press, 1962. pp. 107-48.

Chapter 3

Studies of the MMPI

At the start of the screening program, Bier's modification of the MMPI was chosen as the personality test. Because of this, considerable attention has been given in the writer's research to the predictive value of this test and questions of interpretation. As the goal of the screening became broader in scope than mental health alone and some negative results began to accumulate, there was thought of changing to some instrument which is oriented less to the pathological and more to the measurement of normal qualities, such as motivation, responsibility, decisiveness, and so forth, which tell us more about the kind of person we are dealing with and provide more help in subsequent guidance and counseling. Nevertheless, it remains necessary to keep on the lookout for pathological tendencies, and the MMPI seems better for that than its more recent rivals. It has also the advantage of being supported by a large body of research.

Bier's Modification

Bier made his first revision of the MMPI in 1949, the description of which may be found in some mimeographed sheets he distributed and in Skrincosky's thesis (1952). This was the version used in the screening program until 1956. A further revision appeared in 1955. Although this is described in Barry's thesis (1960) and also in some mimeographed sheets, the relative inaccessibility of these sources makes it advisable to devote space here to its description.

All statements beyond #366 have been dropped, except for the K items, which have been transferred to earlier positions, replacing those eliminated. Two have been changed:

    65 I love my father. (Original: I loved my father.)
  220 I love my mother. (Original: I loved my mother.)

The following are the substitutions:

Dropped	Substituted	Dropped	Substituted	Dropped	Substituted
11	403	70	525	206	442
14	461*	74	463	208	440
15	544	95	445	215	520
17	547	98	450	231	556
20	443	101	493	249	385
27	390	113	398*	258	502*
37	382	115	537	285	446
38	501	133	563	302	382 (=37)
45	383*	167	487	310	443 (=20)
49	397*	177	482	311	501 (=38)
50	374	184	406*	314	544 (=15)
53	407	199	377		
58	379	205	396		

    * K items

The above items were dropped because they created difficulty for religious groups and did not discriminate between the well- and the poorly-adjusted seminarians in Bier's 1948 study. The substituted items (1) were discriminating, (2) seemed to fit the scales to which the dropped items belong, as regards both content and direction of scoring.

The degree to which the scales have been changed is indicated by the following table:

Scale	No. Changed		Scale	No. Changed
L	3		Mf (Male)	5
F	15		Mf (Female)	6
K	0*		Pa	2
Hs	0		Pt	1
D	5		Sc	6
Hy	0		Ma	3
Pd	5		Si	21

* Only two items remain on the reverse side of the answer sheet; all the rest have been transferred to the front.

According to Bier's procedure, the MMPI is scored with the original stencils supplied by the publishers, except for K, which simply requires making a new stencil for the first side of the answer sheet. He had advised caution in the use of the D, Pd, and Mf scales. The published norms were followed. Meanwhile, he accumulated data for revised norms, which he distributed to users of his test in 1958. His position apparently has been that the substituted items fit the scales in which they are inserted, but that a correction must and can be made by the development of special norms for seminary groups. At any rate, in our screening program the clinical scales (Hs to Ma inclusive) were originally scored by means of the published keys without change. The K-scale stencil was corrected: the F-scale stencil was not. L was simply not scored from 1950-1954, but was for most of the 1955 and all of the 1956 candidates. (For the latter two groups, the key was corrected but not the norms: i.e., except as indicated in the following paragraph.)

Special Norms

When the further revision became available toward the end of 1955, it was adopted and the same scoring procedure was used for want of anything better. However, it seemed imperative to the writer to correct all his scales, removing those items which had been changed, except for #65 and 220, in which the substitution of present for past tense introduces no real error. This, of course, meant that new norms had to be developed. This was done tentatively with the protocols from the 1956 group, and the norms were revised each year for four years, at which time the means and standard deviations seemed to have stabilized sufficiently. The final norms are based on 297 cases. The regular MMPI scales are represented, as are also Si, B (Fricke's acquiescence scale), C (Cuadra's Cn, control scale), A (Welsh's first factor, R (Welsh's second factor), and SD (social desirability after Edwards). (Further information on these latter scales may be found in Appendix B.) The subjects included both those who were admitted to the novitiate and those who did not enter. They were all candidates for the priesthood. The K correction was not added because the writer is not convinced that it aids differential diagnosis rather than hinders it.

These norms have been used with all classes from 1963 to the present, and also with candidates for the brothers. Previous records (i.e., from 1956 to 1962) have been corrected for the final norms in preparing them for the research on various aspects of the MMPI. No such correction was attempted for the records before 1956, since the change of form had made it impossible to combine the earlier and the later data. It is, of course, a pity when we are desperately looking for a sufficient number of cases that fall into the various profile types. The norms are presented in Appendix C.

Linear vs. Normalized T Scores

In their standardization, Hathaway and McKinley had chosen to use linear $\underline{T}$ scores (Dahlstrom and Welsh, 1960, p. 17). While the various scales are thus equated for mean and dispersion from the mean when the distribution of scores follows the normal curve, there is a problem when the distribution departs considerably from the normal and differs from scale to scale, as it does in the MMPI (Hathaway and McKinley, 1942; McKinley and Hathaway, 1940, 1942, 1944). A $\underline{T}$ score of 70, for example, may mean a deviation equalled or exceeded by approximately three per cent of the normative group on one scale and five per cent on another. For the purposes of some statistical procedures, Hathaway later (Dahlstrom and Welsh, 1960, p. 259) devised a rough, approximate method of converting his $\underline{T}$ scores to normalized, single-digit scores; but the computation of normalized scores directly from the raw scores was not attempted.

Since profile analysis, particularly according to coding methods which emphasize the first one or two highest scores, is common practice with the MMPI, the writer felt that normalizing might result in profiles more accurately representative of the relative dominance of each scale for the subjects tested. If, for example, a high percentage of subjects earns a linear $\underline{T}$ score of 70 or more on Ma (Hypomania), this scale will tend to be highest more often than some other scale in which the percentage reaching 70 is smaller; thus Hypomania will tend to appear more significant than it really is—at least according to the criterion of frequency of occurrence. Normalization would provide a built-in correction for frequency. Another aspect of the matter was peculiar to the situation at hand: Since special norms had been computed for the applicants to a religious order and the standard deviations of the raw scores were usually a bit lower than those for Hathaway's normative group (as was to be expected with a relatively restricted population), the $\underline{T}$ scores increased by larger steps and the extreme scores tended to be exaggerated. Normalization would also correct this tendency.

Both types of scores were, therefore, derived from 297 test protocols obtained from applicants for four successive years (Weisgerber, 1965; and see Appendix C). This was the entire group, except for a few who were excluded for one of the following reasons: (1) They had not been tested. (2) They had omitted too many items. (3) They had taken the wrong form of the MMPI. (4) The writer could not be certain about the form. The actual comparison of the scoring methods, however, was based on 228 who had been admitted to the novitiate. At the time the data were analyzed, the first of the four classes had completed seven years in the religious life (those, of course, who persevered); the fourth class had completed four years. The criterion of success was taken as perseverance; failure, as leaving.

A computer was used to print out the two sets of scores for each subject on adjacent lines for easy comparison. The profiles were then coded according to Welsh's (Dahlstrom and Welsh, 1960, pp. 19 ff.) method, slightly modified. Inspection of the profiles indicated very little difference between the two sets of scores, so that it appeared superfluous to compute correlations for all pairs. However, twenty were selected as representing about equally both typical instances of near-identity and the most notable differences. Rank-order ($\underline{Rho}$) correlations ranged from .912 to 1.00, with a median of .991; product-moment correlations ($\underline{r}$) ranged from .975 to .996, with a median of .993. These confirm the impression that the profiles are practically identical. The high $\underline{Rho}$ correlations indicate that the rank order of the scales, from highest to lowest, remains pretty much the same for each individual. The $\underline{r}$'s, which by force of the method of computation take into account the actual numerical values of the two scores on the same scale, indicate that the difference is seldom very great. Small differences will probably not influence the clinical interpretation to any extent.

The coding system[1] provided a check of changes in type of profile, defined according to the first, second, and third scales (i.e., the highest, second-highest, and third-highest). The results are shown in Table 3.1. Exact agree-

Table 3.1

Changes in Code Type with Use of Normalized
as against Linear T Scores

	Agreement			Different
Scales	*Complete*	*Substantial*	*At Least Substantial*	
First	85.1%	8.8%	93.9%	6.1%
First Two	70.2	21.5	91.7	8.3
First Three	52.2	36.4	88.6	11.4

ment in regard to the first coded scale is 85 per cent, but it declines to 70 and 52 when the second and third scales are included. However, substantial agreement remains roughly the same: 94, 92, and 89 per cent. (Substantial agreement was reckoned if the original order of scales could be restored with no more than a change of one point in one scale. The "original order" is that found with the linear scores.) Again, the use of normalized scores makes very little difference.

The general height of the profile is also of importance for interpreting the MMPI, particularly scores of 70 or higher. Table 3.2 presents an analysis of the data from this standpoint. Normalization results in slightly fewer profiles that get into the markedly deviant range, but the difference is not great enough to have any practical significance. However, it may have some theoretical importance. The subjects are generally pretty normal according to ratings obtained at the end of the novitiate, which entails extended counseling and very careful scrutiny of their behavior. Hathaway and Meehl (1951) state that 15 per cent of normals have profiles in which at least one score is 70 or above. Normalized scores give us a figure of 17 per cent for our group, which seems more plausible than the 22 per cent by the linear scores. A point not shown in the table is that the degree of deviance is lower; but this is due principally to the fact that the maximum score in this system is 80.

Table 3.2

Effect of Normalizing on Scores at or above 70

No. of Scales	No. of Cases		Percentages*	
	Linear	Normalized	Linear	Normalized
1	33	28	14.5	12.3
2	11	7	4.8	3.1
3	4	1	1.8	0.4
4-6	3	2	1.3	0.9
Total	51	38	22.4	16.7

* These are percentages of the whole group.

The major concern of the writer was to improve the predictive efficiency of the MMPI. Hence, the records of those who persevered and those who dropped out were compared in regard to their first coded scale. The results, presented in Table 3.3, show that there is no great differ-

Table 3.3

Effect of Normalization on Discriminating Power
of Profiles: by Highest Scale

Highest Scale	N	Linear T Scores Per Cent Stayed	Improve-ment	N	Normalized T Scores Per Cent Stayed	Improve-ment
1 (Hs)	19	63.2	0.0	16	62.5	-0.7
2 (D)	19	68.4	5.2	19	68.4	5.2
3 (Hy)	21	71.4	8.2	20	70.0	6.8
4 (Pd)	23	26.1	-37.1	24	29.2	-34.0
5 (Mf)	22	54.5	-8.7	25	64.0	0.8
6 (Pa)	27	70.4	7.2	26	73.1	9.9
7 (Pt)	9	66.7	3.5	6	83.3	20.1
8 (Sc)	11	81.8	18.6	10	80.0	16.8
9 (Ma)	32	68.8	5.6	31	67.7	4.5
0 (Si)	27	55.6	-7.6	26	53.8	-9.4
Ties	18	72.2		25	60.0	

Note--The best estimate of the base rate for staying is probably 63.2 per cent, which is taken from the original 242 subjects. Improvement is computed by subtracting this from the obtained percentage.

ence between the two methods in regard to the predictive power of the highest scale. Only two show any real promise as predictors: Scale 4 (Pd) as a negative indicator and 8 (Sc) as a positive. In both cases the normalized scores would lower the number of correct predictions. Scale 7 (Pt), which appears good according to the results with normalized scores, can hardly be considered because of the small number of cases. It will be noted also in the table that the number of ties is increased by normalization.

Tests of statistical significance have been omitted because they do not appear pertinent to the problem. Whatever random or systematic error is present in the data remains the same for the two types of scores. Nor is there question of estimating parameters from sample data, but rather of comparing two mathematical manipulations of the same data. Replication would seem to be the only sure way of determining to what extent the results can be generalized to other groups or other tests.

In summary, the conclusions are:

1 Normalized T scores with the MMPI give essentially the same results as linear T scores.

2 If they have any advantage, it is in reducing the number of deviant profiles and the extent of the deviation.

3 But this advantage would be offset by a decrease in predictive value.

Results with the MMPI--Earlier Study

In an earlier study (Weisgerber, 1962) considerable attention was given to the MMPI because it was the only personality test that had been used routinely for the first six years of the screening program; and rather strenuous efforts were made to tease out whatever information might be contained in the data. The earlier of Bier's versions had been used; the scoring and norms have been described at the beginning of this chapter.

The subjects were the first five classes screened, i.e., 1950-1954. The original number was 213, but three test records have somehow been lost, one man was excluded because he belonged to a foreign-language mission and could not be followed-up readily; another because he later decided to become a brother in the same order. However, this was substantially the entire group. At the time of this study, those who persevered in the first class had been in the order 11 years; in the fifth class, 7 years; the average was 9 years. Of these 139 had persevered, 69 had left.

Means

The first step was to compare the means of the two groups as in Table 3.4. It is at once apparent that those who persevered did not differ from those who left by even as much as

Table 3.4

MMPI Mean Scores of Those Who Persevered and Those Who Left

| | Raw Scores | | | | T Score Equivalents of Means* | |
| | Persevered (N=139) | | Left (N=69) | | Persev. | Left |
Scale	Mean	S.D.	Mean	S.D.		
F**	8.72	1.92	8.93	2.04	63.44	63.86
K	18.23	4.10	17.57	4.49	61.23	60.14
Hs	12.37	2.56	11.94	2.84	52.74	51.82
D	18.81	2.93	18.42	3.23	55.43	54.26
Hy	20.54	3.66	20.67	4.23	57.08	57.34
Pd	24.32	3.54	24.65	3.14	62.64	63.30
Mf	29.33	4.46	29.74	5.73	67.66	68.48
Pa	9.48	2.50	9.42	2.41	54.44	54.26
Pt	26.00	4.20	25.71	3.77	56.00	55.42
Sc	28.32	4.07	27.87	4.35	61.64	60.64
Ma	19.42	3.76	19.68	3.61	56.26	57.04

* Decimal places determined by interpolation.
** K correction used throughout where appropriate. None of the differences of means approach significance.

one full raw-score point on any of the scales. Except for Ma, the means are higher than those reported by Bier (1948) for both seminary and college samples. The F scale was changed so much in the revision that it is perhaps best ignored or should not have been scored in the first place. While the high K may indicate defensiveness; on the other hand, it is more likely, according to the literature, to indicate good adjustment. But this point will be taken up at greater length later in this chapter. As to the other scales, which have greater clinical significance, it may be noted that Mf, Pd, and Sc are the highest. What this may mean in terms of the typical religious seminarian we

shall consider later, in a section on profile types. The
other means are so close to those of college samples
(Applezweig, 1953; Brown, 1948) that it would be hair-
splitting to discuss them. One thing seems to be rather
painfully clear: if we judge by the means, the MMPI does
not discriminate the successful (persevering) religious
from the unsuccessful. Originally, similar comparisons had
been contemplated after the subjects had been grouped according to the criteria of mental health and overall adjustment. But this did not seem worth the labor in view of
the disappointing results with the simpler criterion and
also the finding, to be indicated later, that other MMPI
indices fared about the same with both types of criteria.

Profile Analysis

That the two groups do not differ appreciably in their
mean scores does not, however, imply that the MMPI is useless. In fact, there is a fundamental objection to the re-
liance on mean scores in a personality test which purports
to measure a number of traits which are more or less distinct.
Let us suppose, by way of illustration, that one person is
clearly depressed but not at all paranoid, while another is
quite paranoid but not depressed. We should expect the first
man to get a high score for D (Depression) and a low score
for Pa (Paranoia); the second man, a low D and a high Pa.
When their scores are averaged, both D and Pa will be intermediate and within the normal range, although both men are
anything but normal, their abnormality being--shall we say?
--selective. And it is precisely one of the advantages of a
"multiphasic" test that it takes account of this selective
abnormality by measuring a group of traits. Hence, the users
of the MMPI have stressed profile analysis, that is, the
consideration of the pattern of scores, with particular attention to which ones are highest. In research, pattern
analysis is most conveniently done by means of a coding
system. Hathaway's method[2] was used in this study. The
profiles were coded, and the groups were compared with
reference to the highest and second-highest scales--or the
first and second coded scales.

Table 3.5 shows the type of profiles tabulated according to the first-coded scale. Some profile types are so
rare among these candidates that they do not provide much
evidence regarding their significance, except perhaps that
their rarity may indicate that the subjects are unlike the
typical religious candidate. In this and the following
tables, the number of cases with each type of profile is
indicated in the column headed "<u>N</u>." Only the types: 4, 5,

Table 3.5

Profile Types (First Coded Scale) in Relation to
    Three Criteria

		Perseverance		Mental Health		Overall Adjust
Code	N*	Per Cent Persevered	N	Per Cent Satisfactory	N	Per Cent Satisfacto
--**	1	100.0	0		0	
1 (Hs)	0		0		0	
2 (D)	1	100.0	1	100.0	1	100.0
3 (Hy)	3	33.3	3	66.7	3	33.3
4 (Pd)	38	68.4	35	74.3	38	63.2
5 (Mf)	95	64.2	88	72.7	91	61.5
6 (Pa)	2	100.0	2	100.0	2	100.0
7 (Pt)	3	100.0	3	100.0	3	100.0
8 (Sc)	26	73.1	26	69.2	26	61.5
9 (Ma)	21	66.7	19	78.9	20	60.0
Ties	18	61.1	17	82.4	17	76.5
No test	3	66.7	3	66.7	3	66.7
Total	211	66.8	197	74.6	204	63.7

    * Numbers of cases do not correspond for the three
criteria because it was not always possible to get adequate
information.
    ** This symbol (--) means that no score was higher than
54.

8, and 9 occur often enough to provide somewhat reliable
percentages. In the bottom line of Table 3.5, are to be
found the percentages for perseverance, satisfactory mental
health, and satisfactory overall adjustment respectively,
of the entire group. These are the base rates as they were
at the time of this study. They do not correspond to those
given in Table 2.5 (and others) in Chapter 2 because the
data for that chapter were brought up to date, whereas it
was not feasible to do so with the present data. Hence,
the old rates were retained as the proper basis of evaluating
the percentages given in the body of the table. (This policy will be followed throughout the book; that is, the base
rates quoted will be those that prevailed for the group of
subjects in question at the time the particular study was
made. There is no other way to avoid constant revision of
the whole body of data every few months.)

The criteria referred to are the same as those described in Chapter 2; the information and method of classification are also the same, except that there was no correction for any change in status after the 1962 study was completed. The percentages satisfactory in regard to mental health are generally higher than for the other two criteria. This is due to the fact that difficulties in adjusting or persevering do not necessarily imply poor mental health. The Scale 3 (Hy) type would, at first sight, seem to be indicative of a poor risk as to perseverance and adjustment; but the results are based on only three cases. Similarly, the four figures of 100 per cent look good, until one notes the number of cases. It is clear that none of the profile types in Table 3.5 has much relation to the criteria. (However, the data presented with reference to normalized scores, and others to be considered later, yield a slightly different picture.)

The first-coded scale, of course, is far from the only feature of the profile that one looks at. However, unless there are thousands of cases to draw from, it is impossible to get enough instances of each combination to draw valid conclusions about the rarer types. The profiles were studied for the various combinations of the two highest (or first two coded) scales, but only a few were frequent enough to be worth discussing. These are shown in Table 3.6. The 54

Table 3.6

Most Common Profile Types (by First Two Coded Scales) in Relation to Three Criteria

		Perseverance		Mental Health		Overall Adjustment
Code	N	Per Cent Persevered	N	Per Cent Satisfactory	N	Per Cent Satisfactory
45	10	70.0	9	77.8	10	80.0
48	10	60.0	9	77.8	10	50.0
52	12	75.0	11	90.9	12	75.0
53	10	70.0	9	66.7	9	66.7
54	32	65.6	31	67.7	32	62.5
58	13	69.2	11	72.7	12	58.3
59	8	37.5	8	87.5	8	50.0
84	9	66.7	9	66.7	9	66.7
94	8	62.5	7	71.4	8	62.5
Base Rate		66.8		74.6		63.7

(Mf, Pd) pattern is the only one which is common enough, but it does not show percentages appreciably different from the base rate. According to the criteria of perseverance and overall adjustment, 59 (Mf, Ma) and possibly 48 (Pd, Sc) may deserve attention in future research.

In the previous analyses, similar two-digit codes have been treated as though they were completely unrelated, v.g., 45 and 54, although actually a difference of only a few points may determine which scale is first or second. Furthermore, inspection of the profiles suggested that, when 4 is not only first but also quite high, it may have greater significance. It was also hoped that combining similar types might provide a sufficient number of cases to work with. Hence, a search was made for various combinations which might show some promise. The results are to be found in Table 3.7. The percentages, as in the two preceding tables, are given in terms of the positive (i.e., satisfactory) pole of the respective criteria; but it is how much <u>lower</u> they are than the base rate that is of interest.

Table 3.7

Most Predictive Code Combinations in Relation to
    Three Criteria

			Satisfactory	
Code Combination	N[a]	Persevered[b]	Mental Health	Overall Adjustmen
59	8	<u>37.5%</u>	87.5%	50.0%
59 or 95, without ties	13	<u>38.5</u>	75.0	41.7
59, 5⌒9, or 95[c]	14	<u>42.9</u>	76.9	46.2
94 or 49	10	50.0	66.7	50.0
94, 49, 4⌒9, 59, 5⌒9, 95	29	51.7	74.1	53.6
4, 5, & 9 in first three	24	54.2	69.6	58.3
4', including ties for first	24	58.3	69.6	54.2
48	10	60.0	77.8	50.0
94, 4⌒9, or 49	15	60.0	71.4	60.0
Base rate		66.8	74.6	63.7

    a To save space, the total numbers of cases are given only for the perseverance criterion; discrepancies from these totals in regard to the other criteria are no more than one or two.
    b The underlining indicates that the percentage differs from the base rate at a probability level of .05 or better.
    c The arc (⌒) joining the two scales indicates a tie. As to 4', this means here that 4 was first and 70 or above; other scales in the profile may also have been 70 or above.

As can be seen, nothing is accomplished in regard to predicting mental health. Although only three combinations achieve statistical significance, and only for the perseverance criterion, it appears that several of the patterns may eventually prove useful predictors. The purely empirical approach taken in the analysis of the data stands out like a sore thumb. For example, the 94 or 49 patterns suggest a 50 per cent chance of perseverance and good adjustment, but the addition of ties ($\widehat{49}$) raises the chance by 10 per cent. Why an apparent balance between these two tendencies (Psychopathic Deviate and Hypomania) should be any better than the two of them in a similar degree is something of a puzzle, unless, of course, this is merely an instance of the reversal of trends one is apt to find when dealing with small samples and measures that are subject to a considerable percentage of error. Nevertheless, some tentative generalizations can be made, subject to test in future research. While the 4, 5, and 9 patterns taken by themselves are the commonest in both good and poor prospects, in certain combinations they indicate poor promise of adjustment and perseverance. The least desirable patterns seem to be those with 5 and 9 as the two highest. Next come those with 4 and 9, although there is some doubt about the matter in view of the ambiguous results with 4 and 9 tied. When 4, 5, and 9 are the first three scales, regardless of their order, the indication is a bit unfavorable; as is also the case when 4 is highest and at a T score of 70 or more. The 48 pattern (Pd, Sc) may also be unfavorable.

All of these conclusions need further verification; they amount to no more than hypotheses suggested by the data at hand in 1962. The writer has done a little checking by adding the data for 1955, although he used only the criterion of perseverance. The results remained substantially the same. From 1956 on, as has previously been indicated, the more recent of Bier's revisions of the MMPI has been used, and the writer has employed his own norms. The special norms automatically correct for the tendency of Scales 4, 5, 9, and 8 to be high; consequently it is impossible to add the later data to the earlier and thus get more cases of each profile type or make a straightforward comparison of the two sets of data. As we shall see in a moment, the unfavorable roles of Scales 4 and 9 are confirmed.

Types of Personality

However, before going on to new data, let us return to the question of the prevailing personality types among candidates for the religious life. The highest means in

Table 3.4 were those for Scales 5 (Mf), 4 (Pd), and 8 (Sc). Table 3.8, which in part duplicates Table 3.5, displays the figures on personality types with particular reference to

Table 3.8

Personality Types According to First Coded Scale of the MMPI

	Number of Cases			Per Cent of Respective Group		
Code	Persev.	Left	Total	Persev.	Left	Total
--	1		1	.7		.4
1	1		1	.7		.4
2	1		1	.7		.4
3	3	3	6	2.0	3.8	2.6
4	33	18	51	21.7	23.1	22.2
5	65	36	101	42.8	46.2	43.9
6	3		3	2.0		1.3
7	4		4	2.6		1.7
8	24	12	36	15.8	15.4	15.6
9	17	9	26	11.2	11.5	11.3
Total	152	78	230	100.2	100.0	99.8

Note--There were 18 cases in which two or more scales were tied for first. In these cases, each such scale was counted as though it stood for a distinct subject. This, of course, is the reason why the numbers in the "Total" row exceed those given in subsequent tables.

the constitution of the group who entered and the two subgroups: those who persevered and those who left. The precise number of cases has been given so that, at least this once, the reader may see how many small numbers are involved and deduce how unreliable some of the percentages must be. The percentages in this table do not immediately refer to the rate of perseverance; rather they indicate what proportion in the whole group and the two subgroups showed a given personality type. Only the first coded scale was used. However, ties were resolved by counting each tied scale as thou it represented a separate case. Although this results in coun ing some subjects twice or even more, it was thought that th solution would result in a truer picture than merely excludi the ties. Except for the types which are very infrequent, th group remains about the same despite attrition. The frequent types are the same as those suggested above in reference to Table 3.4, except that 9 (Ma) must be added.

What do these findings imply regarding the kind of person who is attracted to the religious life and remains in it? Mf is first in 44 per cent of the cases and is the highest mean. Some of the subjects are undoubtedly a bit effeminate in manner, but certainly not such a high percentage--as anyone can attest who has played a contact sport against a team of seminarians. College groups generally tend to be high on this scale (Applezweig, 1953; Brown, 1948); this fact and the content of many of the items suggest the effect of education, especially in regard to literary and artistic interests, as well as general refinement of attitudes and manners. Scale 4 (Pd), which has the next highest mean and is the peak score of 22 per cent of the men, also tends to be high in college students. As to the fact that Sc is highest in about 16 per cent of the cases, no satisfactory explanation is apparent. It is quite possible that these people have a somewhat schizoid personality and were as a consequence attracted by the relatively seclusive and protective aspects of the religious life. But they very soon learn that they cannot seclude themselves from their own group and that their work will bring them in contact with more people and give them more responsibility than would likely have been the case had they chosen family life. Yet they tend to persevere and make a good adjustment. The frequency of the Ma peak, 11 per cent, is easier to understand. Most of the candidates enter right after high school or only a little college work. They are young, immature, perhaps impulsive, and energetic; many of them have been quite active in high-school extracurriculars, in fact often too much so.

Meaning of High Pd Scores

It has been something of a mystery to the writer why Pd, which presumably indicates a tendency to show the characteristics of the classical psychopathic personality, should run so high on the average and be so frequently the highest score in a group of seminarians. It will be helpful to pursue this matter further by considering some data obtained from the 1962 study but not previously analyzed in detail.

In the rating form used for the follow-up (cf. Chapter 2, pp. 16 f.), there is a category for observance of religious discipline, in which the following choices are offered the rater:

_____ Rebellious, trouble-maker, very poor observer,
      and/or irresponsible.
_____ In between.
_____ Good observer, no trouble.
_____ Don't know.

Attempts were made to use this as a three-point rating scale,
despite the fact that it was originally intended simply as
a convenient way of indicating who were quite satisfactory
in this regard and who were not. Thus rectilinear and curvilinear correlations were computed, the distribution of
average ratings was observed, and so forth. These attempts
did not yield a clear picture, probably because of the
coarseness of a three-point scale and the tendency of the
ratings to be favorable--as they should if all is well in
the seminary. Hence, it was decided to base the analysis
on the percentages of those who were rated favorably, i.e.,
"good observer, no trouble." The results are presented in
Table 3.9 with reference to the Pd scores themselves and in
Table 3.10 with reference to profile types. In order to

Table 3.9

Relation of Pd Scores and Ratings for Discipline

| | With K Correction | | Without K Correction | |
| | | Per Cent | | Per Cent |
T Scores	N	Good	N	Good
70---	29	51.7	16	50.0
65-69	42	73.8	20	55.0
60-64	70	61.4	44	68.2
55-59	22	72.7	65	67.7
50-54	18	72.2	28	57.1
---49	8	75.0	16	93.8
Total	189	65.6	189	65.6

Note--Maximum $\underline{T}$ score with 88 with K and 83 without;
minimum, 43 and 42 respectively. The score intervals at
the two ends are larger in order to get a larger number
of cases at these extremes.

Table 3.10

Profile Type and Discipline

Code	N	Per Cent Good
2	1	100.0
3	3	33.3
4	32	56.2
5	86	72.1
6	2	50.0
7	3	100.0
8	26	50.0
9	18	61.1
4'	17	41.2
49, 49, 94	14	57.1
Base rate		65.6

Note--The 4' means that 4 was first and at least 70.

minimize the usual difficulty arising from small numbers of cases at both ends of such distributions, the top interval is 70 and above, while the bottom interval is up to 49. The trend of the data would look a bit more regular if the intermediate intervals had consisted of ten points, but the dividing lines chosen are significant in the clincal interpretation of the MMPI, and the irregularity should probably not be smoothed away. A comparison of the results with and without the K correction supports to some extent the writer's skepticism about the value of the correction. Without it there is a definite drop in the percentages of those rated good, when the $\underline{T}$ score reaches 65 or more. It is true that there is an embarrassing inversion of the trend of the data at 50-54, but one usually is more concerned about the high scores. At any rate, of those with a score of 70 or more, about 50 per cent are satisfactory as against a base rate of 65.6.

In Table 3.10 the profile types according to the first coded scale are given and then two combinations; others were considered but omitted because they were found in less than ten cases. Ignoring those for which there were only a few subjects, we find that the Scale 8 type of profile shows up poorly; this is surprising and a little hard to explain. However, the role of Scale 4 makes sense. If it is the highest one, 56 per cent are satisfactory; if it is 70 or more, whether first or not, 50-52 per cent; if both first and 70 or more (4' in Table 3.10), 41 per cent. As in previous analyses, the combination of 4 and 9 as the first two highest scales is somewhat unfavorable.

Do these findings tend to confirm the validity of Pd as a measure of psychopathic tendency or some such characteristic? They provide positive evidence only with regard to those cases in which the score is quite high in itself or relatively to the other scales or, especially, both together. The fact that lower scores do not show any clearcut, direct relation to observance of religious discipline poses no insuperable difficulty for the position that the scale is valid all along the line. Other personality traits, reflected in other scales, may well act as control factors, particularly when the Pd tendency is of moderate intensity and overshadowed by these other traits.

The implication, then, would be that a sizeable proportion of the seminarians have at least a tendency in common with the psychopathic deviate. They had not given expression to this in any serious way previously or they would not have been admitted. Although it does not ordinarily find expression in behavior comparable to that of the classic psychopath, it poses a problem if it is notably above normal or is not balanced by other factors. Roughly about half who fall into these last categories have some trouble with religious discipline. In the 1962 study the suggestion was made that Pd may reflect an independence which can be either healthy or unhealthy. This interpretation is not inconsistent with the present data; in fact such independence may be the common element referred to above, and the present data may be seen as indicating that it does indeed often become unhealthy.

Later Classes--1956-1962

We shall be able to return to the question of relating profile types to the criteria of perseverance or adjustment when we consider later classes. However, the new data will not permit us to make any further statements about personality types among these young men. The use of the regular MMPI norms has, in effect, provided us with control groups: the normative population and the college groups used in various published studies. This has been precluded by the decision to use special, seminary norms. As it is, objection can be taken to data in Table 3.8 because Bier had introduced some changes into almost all the scales and thus had made the use of the published norms, strictly speaking, inappropriate.

The reason for passing over the 1955 class has been given earlier. Since Bier's 1955 revision was used with all classes from 1956 on, later studies of the MMPI must be kept distinct from the preceding, except for K. The following section will concern data from those who entered the novitiate from 1956-1962.

These seven classes were in the order long enough for a reasonably good follow-up. Since various aspects of the analysis were performed at different times, as opportunity permitted, the length of the follow-up period was not the same for all the variables which will be described. When these analyses were begun, the length of the period was a little over two years for the latest class and a little over eight years for the earliest. The group was divided into two for the purposes of cross-validation. The last three classes (1960-1962) were taken for the initial survey; the first four (1956-1959) for the cross-validation. This choice, which is a bit unusual, was really an accident. For various reasons which he does not now recall clearly the writer started with the 1960-1962 group and later decided to use the earlier group for cross-validation. The classes could have been divided according to alternate groups, but there is reason for suspecting that some trends persist for a few years and then are reversed. For convenience we shall use the terms *Group I* for 1960-1962 and *Group II* for 1956-1959.

It will be seen when the tables of results are presented that the number of cases varies somewhat. The maxima were 166 in Group I, 227 in Group II, and 388 for the total. Some subjects had to be excluded because they were not given the test, some because the older version was used, one because of test invalidity. However, the main reason was that the study stretched over almost two years, and meanwhile various men left the order at different times. When the reason for leaving was either poor physical health or lack of academic success, these men were excluded from the tabulations, since these conditions did not seem pertinent to the objective of screening, which concerned adjustment and mental health. As various men left, it was not feasible to be harrying the busy superiors to find out the reason; these men were reluctantly excluded--reluctantly because some useful data were probably lost in this way.

In most of the analyses perseverance is the criterion of success. The use of this criterion has been discussed before: it is not the most desirable, but it yields results similar to those obtained with the criteria of adjustment and mental health. The source of information on adjustment, when it is used as the point of reference, has been indicated in Chapter 2; and so for the method of classification.

In view of the results of the earlier study (cf. Table 3.4), there was no point in computing the mean scores of those who persevered and those who left. The profiles were again coded, but the system was changed to that devised by Welsh (Dahlstrom and Welsh, 1960, pp. 19 ff.), with a slight modification. The first-coded scales are displayed in Table 3.11. As previously, the "Total" row at the bottom represents

Table 3.11

Relation of High-Point Code to Perseverance

Code	Group I		Group II		Total	
	N	Persev.	N	Persev.	N	Persev.
1	10	40.0%	17	64.7%	27	55.6%
2	16	62.5	19	68.4	35	65.7
3	22	63.6	21	71.4	43	67.4
4	16	62.5	23	17.4	39	35.9
5	12	66.7	22	54.6	34	58.8
6	21	61.9	25	68.0	46	65.2
7	13	46.2	8	62.5	21	52.4
8	11	36.4	10	80.0	21	57.1
9	20	40.0	31	67.7	51	56.9
0	12	50.0	27	55.6	39	53.8
Ties	13	38.5	17	70.6	30	56.7
Total	166	53.3	220	59.3	386	56.6

the base rate. The percentages, however, are taken, not just from those subjects included in this table, but from the entire group, exclusive only of those who had left because of academic deficiencies or for reasons unknown, at the time, to the author. Comparison of Groups I and II reveals that no one high point is consistently bad. However, a high on Scale 4 (Pd) shows such a low rate of perseverance in Group II and consequently in the total group that it seems to be worthy of further study. As to favorable indicators, 2 (D), 3 (Hy), and 6 (Pa) seem to be of some use.

The low points of the profiles are also of interest and are given in Table 3.12. The first thing to be noted is that these are concentrated a little more than the high points, particularly on Scales 2, 3, and 9 (Ma). The unfavorable lows are not very clear: only Scale 6 shows any consistency from one group to the next, and the improvement over the base rate is rather slight. On the favorable side, Scales 2, 7 (Pt), and 8 (Sc) show some promise.

Table 3.12

Relation of Low-Point Code to Perseverance

| | Group I | | Group II | | Total | |
Code	N	Persev.	N	Persev.	N	Persev.
1	4	0.0%	15	53.3%	19	42.1%
2	27	59.3	20	80.0	47	68.1
3	23	34.8	28	60.7	51	49.0
4	8	37.5	21	61.9	29	55.2
5	19	52.6	19	42.1	38	47.4
6	17	47.1	20	50.0	37	48.6
7	4	100.0	10	80.0	14	85.7
8	6	66.7	14	78.6	20	75.0
9	25	56.0	38	65.8	63	61.9
0	18	55.6	13	38.5	31	48.4
Ties	15	73.3	22	54.6	37	62.2
Total	166	53.3	220	59.3	386	56.6

Attention was not restricted to the highest or lowest scores alone. The second highest was also considered, but the number of cases was generally so small that only a few combinations could be selected as worth reporting. Consideration was also given to the second lowest scale, but the number of cases was entirely too small. Further, a tabulation was made of the combination of high and low points; again, the plague of small numbers. Lastly, attention was centered on the cases in which Scale 4 was highest, among the highest, or paired with Scale 9. Only the combinations involving 10 or more cases are reported here (Table 3.13). These data are taken from the total group.

The unfavorable patterns, if we prescind from the small Ns are 4' (Pd at 70 or above), 20, 63, 49 or 94, and generally the presence of Scale 4 in the first two. The finding that makes best sense in these data is the role of Scale 4, which is supposed to indicate irresponsibility, rebelliousness, and behavior akin to that of the so-called psychopath or sociopath. When it is at least the second highest, it suggests at best about a fifty-fifty chance of perseverance. When it is first--and not necessarily very high absolutely-- the chances drop to just a little better than one in three (according to the data in Table 3.11). When it reaches or exceeds 70, the situation becomes a bit worse. A high point also on Scale 9 seems to confirm Scale 4, but does not reduce the chances of perseverance appreciably.

Table 3.13

Various Code Combinations and Perseverance

Code*	N	Persevered
20	10	40.0%
36	10	60.0
63	10	40.0
94	13	46.2
4' (first or tied)	10	30.0
4' (first or not)	15	33.3
4 second	39	48.7
4 in first two**	87	49.4
49 or 94	17	47.1
6---2	15	73.3
2—-9	16	68.8
Base rate		56.6

* The 4' means that Scale 4 was 70 or above. Code 6---2 means that Scale 6 was highest and 2 was lowest; and similarly for 2---9.

** Includes instances in which Scale 4 was tied for second.

The favorable combinations are 36, 6---2 (6 highest and 2 lowest), and 2---9 (2 highest and 9 lowest). The contrast in perseverance rates for 36 and 63 is curious and probably should prompt one to caution. After all, to change the profile from 36 to 63 would require just a difference of a point or two. The role of Scale 2 is interesting. If we examine the data on this scale in Tables 3.11--3.13, we find it a favorable indicator when it is the high point (except for the 20 pattern) and when it is the low point, particularly in the 6---2 combination. This suggests a curvilinear relationship, i.e., with both high and low scores favorable but intermediate scores unfavorable or neutral. This would indeed be strange, since a high score should indicate at least a tendency to depression. A check of this hypothesis was made by tabulating the scores of Group II against perseverance. The relationship appeared linear and inverse, i.e., the perseverance rate was better with low scores and decreased as D became progressively higher. Biserial correlation was then computed and the result was -.145. No doubt the role of this scale is complex; perhaps it is measuring something else besides depression.

Scale 9 is unfavorable when it is conjoined with 4 as one of the high points, but favorable when it is the low point and 2 is the high point. But we shall give further attention to this scale later.

Some of the indicators discussed above are not very decisive in terms of degree of improvement over the base rate, and one may object that some of these results may easily be due to the operation of chance factors. On the other hand, it will be noted that findings with regard to the patterns involving Scales 4 and 9 are in essential agreement with those in the 1962 study.

The K Scale

Earlier in this chapter note was taken of the fact that the mean $\underline{T}$ score of the 1950–1954 group was high (61) on K, and the question was raised whether the scale really measures defensiveness or adjustment. Dahlstrom and Welsh (1960, pp. 142–50) have reviewed the literature very thoroughly and show that the matter is rather complicated. Some of the earlier research of the writer suggested a curvilinear relation to adjustment; this would tend to fit with the idea that K does indeed measure adjustment, except for extremely high scores, which would be indicative of defensiveness. However, the data could not be accepted with much confidence because the number of cases at the extreme scores was quite small. Fortunately for our purposes, both of Bier's revisions leave this scale intact, except for the transfer to earlier positions of items originally occurring after #366; and consequently we can combine all of our data. This has been done in Table 3.14.

Table 3.14

Relation of K Scale to Overall Adjustment

		Per Cent Satisfactorily Adjusted				
*K Score**	*N*	*1950–1954*	*N*	*1955–1962*	*N*	*1950–1962*
26–29	9	44.4	4	75.0	13	53.8
22–25	34	64.7	86	65.1	120	65.0
18–21	62	71.0	130	59.2	192	63.0
14–17	68	57.4	142	50.0	210	52.4
10–13	21	76.2	57	45.6	78	53.8
6–9	7	42.9	14	28.6	21	33.3
Total	201	63.7	433	54.7	634	57.6

 * Raw scores.

In exception to the general rule, the 1955 group is included, although it does not affect the results appreciably. The curvilinear relation shown by the 1950-1954 group is negated by a clearly linear relation in the later group. The curve appears again when the 1950-1962 years are taken together, but this is obviously due to the preponderance of the earlier group in the top score-interval. One thing is rather clear: very low scores, i.e., below 10, are not associated with good adjustment.

With Table 3.15 we return to our pattern of Group I (1960-1962) for the initial analysis and Group II (1956-1959) for cross-validation. The criterion is again perse-

Table 3.15

Relation of K Scale to Perseverance

| T Score | Group I | | Group II | | Total | |
	N	Persev.	N	Persev.	N	Persev.
70-79	1	100.0%	4	50.0%	5	60.0%
60-69	30	63.3	45	66.7	75	65.3
50-59	49	57.1	64	59.4	113	58.4
40-49	55	54.6	76	59.2	131	57.3
30-39	24	33.3	26	61.5	50	48.0
20-29	7	28.6	5	40.0	12	33.3

verance. The results are as conflicting as the preceding: while the first group shows an increase in perseverance rate with increase of K score, the second gives the impression of a curvilinear relation, except for some irregularity in the middle ranges, 30-69. And we have the same problem as above with the data for the combined group. However, again the low scores seem consistently to indicate a poor chance of perseverance: overall, only one-third of those who have a T score below 30 persevere in their vocation.

The SD Scale

In view of the demonstrated importance of response sets in personality inventories like the MMPI, Edwards' measure of Social Desirability (SD) has been employed (1957, pp. 27-39). Since this scale is similar in meaning to the original intent of K and the two have shown high correlations (Dahlstrom and Welsh, 1960, pp. 142-45; Edwards, 1957, p. 44), it was thought that some improvement in prediction might be gained by using these scales in combination. A particular hypothesis which guided the investigation—although it could not properly be tested with the data at hand—was that high K with low SD might indicate that K was in some cases reflecting good adjustment, with the social desirability factor eliminated. The procedure was to make a double contingency table, with each cell representing a given level of K and SD; then the perseverance percentage was computed for the cases in the cell. The results are given in Table 3.16. Table 3.17 is similar, ex-

Table 3.16

Relation of K and SD to Perseverance

Group I:

K Score	*N*	*--24*	SD Score 25-29	*30-32*	*Total*
22 --	30		75.0	65.4	66.7
18-21	47		47.6	53.8	51.1
14-17	54	66.7	48.7	77.8	55.6
-- 13	30	37.5	25.0	0.0	30.0
Total	161	45.4	46.1	60.3	51.6

Group II:

K Score	*N*	*--24*	SD Score 25-29	*30-32*	*Total*
22 --	50	100.0	60.0	56.4	58.0
18-21	67		58.6	55.3	56.7
14-17	76	75.0	52.9	47.1	54.0
-- 13	34	38.5	52.4		47.1
Total	227	54.5	55.0	54.3	54.6

Total Group:

K Score	*N*	*--24*	SD Score 25-29	*30-32*	*Total*
22 --	80	100.0	64.3	60.0	61.2
18-21	114		54.0	54.7	54.4
14-17	130	71.4	51.1	57.7	54.6
-- 13	64	37.9	42.4	0.0	39.1
Total	388	50.0	51.3	56.7	53.4

Note—Figures in body of table are per cent who persevered. Where there is a blank, there were no subjects in the category; where the percentage is 0.0, there were some, but all left. Raw scores are used; 22 -- means 22 and above; -- 13 and --24, up to and including 13 and 24 respectively.

77

Table 3.17

Relation of K and SD to Overall Adjustment

Group I:

| | | | SD Score | | |
K Score	N	--24	25-29	30-32	Total
22 --	30		75.0	65.4	66.7
18-21	47		47.6	57.7	53.2
14-17	54	50.0	48.7	77.8	53.7
-- 13	30	31.2	25.0	50.0	30.0
Total	161	36.4	46.1	63.5	51.6

Group II:

22 --	51	100.0	63.6	64.1	64.7
18-21	66		58.6	64.9	62.1
14-17	76	75.0	45.1	47.1	48.7
-- 13	34	38.5	57.1		50.0
Total	227	54.6	52.7	61.3	56.4

Total Group:

22 --	81	100.0	66.7	64.6	65.4
18-21	113		54.0	61.9	58.4
14-17	130	64.3	46.7	57.7	50.8
-- 13	64	34.5	45.5	50.0	40.6
Total	388	45.5	50.0	62.2	54.4

Note--Figures in body of table are per cent who were
satisfactory in regard to overall adjustment. All scores
are raw scores.

cept that the criterion is overall adjustment. In both tables,
the last column, "Total," shows the relation of K alone to
the criterion; this, of course, overlaps in part with the data
given in Table 3.14. The rows labelled "Total" show the predictive fortunes of SD alone. The Ns may be misleading: they
are pertinent only to the percentages in the "Total" column,
for which they were the divisor. The Ns in the main portion
of the table varied considerably: in fact, from one to ninety.
This is a good illustration of one of the drawbacks of a contingency table such as this.

What seems to stand out is that the combination of low
K and low SD makes for both poor adjustment and lack of per-

severance; the percentages are remarkably similar for the
initial and the cross-validation groups. To use the combined
figures, only about 35 per cent are well-adjusted and 38 per
cent persevere. However, low K is almost as successful a predictor alone as in combination with low SD. The latter, by
itself, does not predict perseverance very well, although
it seems to do a little better against the criterion of adjustment.

The A and R Scales

Among the other experimental scales which have been used
are two devised by Welsh (1956) on the basis of factor analysis
and called A (for Anxiety) and R (for Repression). These also
have been studied in relation to one another. The cases were
first divided into high, average, and low on these variables:
high meaning that the $\underline{T}$ score was 60 or above; average, 40–
59; low, less than 40. For the results see Table 3.18. The

Table 3.18

Relation of A and R Scales to Perseverance

Group I:

A Score	N	Low	R Score Aver.	High	Total
High	37	37.5	31.8	57.1	37.8
Aver.	102	50.0	56.2	56.2	54.9
Low	27	66.7	66.7	66.7	66.7
Total	166	48.5	53.3	57.7	53.0

Group II:

	N	Low	Aver.	High	Total
High	27	50.0	44.4	66.7	48.1
Aver.	162	66.7	53.9	60.9	56.8
Low	26	100.0	55.0	50.0	57.7
Total	215	65.6	52.9	60.0	55.8

Total Group:

	N	Low	Aver.	High	Total
High	64	42.9	37.5	60.0	42.2
Aver.	264	58.7	54.7	59.0	56.1
Low	53	80.0	61.0	57.1	62.3
Total	381	56.9	53.1	58.9	54.6

Note--High is $\underline{T}$ score of 60 or above; low is less than
40. Figures in body of table are per cent who persevered.

same comment as above applies to the N̲s listed in the second column as against the N̲s for each cell.

The data suggest that a combination of low A and R makes for perseverance, but the high percentage must be taken with a grain of salt because the number of cases even for the total group was only 5. There is also an indication that high R acts as a moderator on high A, but again the number of cases for the total group was only 10. The possible moderating influence of high R makes sense in relation to the meaning of these scales: anxiety for A and repression for R; it is intelligible that repression would tend to control the effect of anxiety, even though there may be some cost to the individual in the long run. The R scale alone does not seem to have any direct correlation with perseverance. A, on the contrary, shows the inverse relationship we should expect of a measure of anxiety.

The Ma Scale

In some of the writer's earlier work attempts were made to find single MMPI scales which might serve as good predictors, and among these Ma (Scale 9) seemed promising. Its function has already been mentioned in the context of profile analysis; here it is considered with reference to its absolute value rather than its position in relation to other measures. The subjects were grouped according to their T̲ scores, and the percentage of perseverance was determined for each score interval. The results are shown in Table 3.19.

Table 3.19

Relation of Scale 9 to Perseverance

	Group I		Group II		Total	
T Score	*N*	*Persev.*	*N*	*Persev.*	*N*	*Persev.*
70-79	5	40.0%	5	60.0%	10	50.0%
60-69	25	40.0	28	60.7	53	50.9
50-59	57	50.9	61	52.5	118	51.7
40-49	52	57.7	95	61.0	147	59.9
30-39	27	63.0	28	75.0	55	69.1
20-29			3	66.7	3	66.7
Total	166	53.0	220	60.5	386	57.3

The initial group (I) shows a rather clear-cut relation: as the score on this scale increases, the rate of perseverance declines. But this finding does not hold up when cross-validated (Group II), except that the lower scores (below 40) seem to be favorable indicators. Since statistics are generally more reliable with greater numbers of cases, one is inclined to base his final conclusions on the totals for the two groups combined, in which one again gets the same impression as with Group I. However, if looked at in another way, the results point to a problem which recurs in all this work. A few successive classes may be taken as a sample, and some score or characteristic will seem to be a useful predictor. But when this is tested with another set of successive classes, it will not be confirmed or will work only at the low or high end of the continuum. This may be due to the vagaries of relatively small samples. However, another explanation is possible: Each group is somewhat different in the types of individuals it comprises, in homogeneity, in cohesiveness, in *esprit de corps*, in the way it relates to superiors and the way they relate to it, and in many other things. A rather overactive person (high Ma score) may fit in with one group, which is tolerant of such deviates or perhaps well-supplied with kindred souls; he may clash with another group in which tolerance is not so prevalent or in which overactive persons frequently find themselves in conflict with one another over their objectives and ambitions. In short, a predictor may lose its usefulness when the classes change in character.

Barry's Seminary Scale

A special seminary scale, called "Se" and later "Re," was constructed by Barry (1960) in hopes of improving the prediction of fitness for the religious life. He made use of the data on applicants for a religious order over a ten-year period, 1949-1958, assigning the odd-numbered years to the item-analysis group and the even-numbered years to the cross-validation group.

Coelho (1963) attempted a further validation. He encountered some initial problems, which required changes in the scale. The span of years studied by Barry involved the use of both of Bier's revisions of the MMPI: the 1949 and the 1955. Although Barry had intended to eliminate items which were not identical in the two versions, three had been overlooked; these obviously had to be dropped. Difficulty was also encountered with duplicate items, which occur in the MMPI simply for convenience in machine scoring. Eight such pairs of duplicates were found in the Se scale. In four instances, both members of the pair had been scored. Since this practice gave such items double weight and this seemed risky, the second of each pair was dropped. In the remaining

four instances, the statement proved significantly discrim-
inative when it appeared in one position in the MMPI and not
in the other position. This fact cast some doubt on the value
of these items, and they were dropped. Thus the length of the
scale was reduced from 81 to 70 items.

Coelho then applied this modified and, it is hoped, improved scale to the author's MMPI protocols of those who
entered the novitiate in 1950-1958. There was 421 subjects
in all. These men belonged to the same religious order as
Barry's group, but in a different section of the country.
Two criteria were used: overall adjustment and perseverance.
The first criterion was applied only to the 1950-1955 classes;
the second, to all. The results are presented in Table 3.20.

Table 3.20

Se Scores in Relation to Criteria:
   Adjustment and Perseverance

	Mean	*S.D.*	*N*	*Years*
Satisfactory	15.07	7.49	128	1950-1954
Doubtful or Unsatisfactory	14.35	7.10	72	
Persevered	15.26	7.58	274	1950-1958
Left	14.36	6.74	147	

Note—Differences in means are not significant.

It is obvious that the scale does not stand up under
further validation. Higher scores are supposed to indicate
less promise for the seminary or religious life. And Barry
obtained a large and significant difference between his
"good" and "poor" groups in both his original and cross-
validation samples: means of 14.63 and 14.85 for the "good";
23.48 and 22.61 for the "poor." In his classification,
"good" means persevering and hence presumably well-adjusted
to the religious life; therefore, it corresponds to "persevered" in Table 3.20. "Poor" means those who left the seminary at least partly for psychological reasons or were
denied admission because of psychological reasons. While he
maintains that the MMPI was never the principal ground for
rejecting a candidate, it would be hard to show that it did
not influence the decision. Furthermore, there was no test
of the validity of the judgment of unfitness, since these
subjects did not enter the religious life—at least no
confirmatory evidence is reported. Consequently there is

reason to doubt the adequacy of this criterion for part of his "poor" group. This may be the reason for the discrepancy between his and Coelho's results. Nevertheless, one suspects this is merely an instance of a test element which works with one group and not with another--a familiar phenomenon in psychological testing. At any rate, Coelho's results show that those who persevere and those who are satisfactory score about the same as the others and, if anything, a trifle higher, i.e., worse.

A Work-Attitude Scale

Because of its connection with motivation, Tydlaska and Mengel's (1953) Work Attitude scale was tried. There were 29 items retained in the modified MMPI. From the 1956-1962 classes, 62 men had been rated as definitely having good motivation for the religious life and 23, as having poor motivation (cf. Chapter 4). Doubtful cases were excluded. These numbers were so small because this information had not deliberately been sought by the writer but had been volunteered by the master of novices in the routine follow-up. Little attention had originally been given to motivation in the psychological screening because this had been considered primarily the business of the other examiners of the candidates. The protocols of the 85 men were scored for Work Attitude (Wa) and the usual statistics computed.

The difference in means between the well and the poorly motivated groups was not great (1.63 in raw-score units), although it was statistically significant ($\underline{P}$ of .017 for a one-tailed test). Overlap in scores of the two groups was considerable. Some cutting points, nevertheless, could be used with profit; for example, there were 21 who had a score of eight or higher, and 11 of these (52.4 per cent) had poor motivation and 15 (71.4 per cent) left. Although the scale seems to measure motivation to some extent and is related to perseverance, one probably needs something more directly indicative of motivation for the religious life as such.

A number of other experimental scales were investigated from time to time. These will be mentioned briefly in Appendix B.

Conclusions

In this chapter the first thing taken up after the description of Bier's modification of the MMPI was the question of norms. A comparison of linear and normalized $\underline{T}$ scores based on 297 protocols of applicants for the novitiate led to the following conclusions: Normalized and linear $\underline{T}$ scores give essentially the same results. However, normalization reduces the number of deviant profiles and the extent of the deviation, but it also decreases the predictive power of the test.

The results of an earlier study showed that those who persevere in the religious life do not differ from those who leave in their mean scores on the MMPI. Nor were there any differences of moment in regard to profile types, when these were determined by the highest scale. When the second-highest was also considered and some other combinations, the following patterns seemed to be unfavorable indicators, in descending order: Scales 5 (Mf) and 9 (Ma) as the two highest; 4 (Pd) and 9, but not cases in which the two were tied; 4, 5, and 9 as the first three regardless of their order; 4 highest and at a T score of 70 or above; and perhaps also 4 and 8 (Sc) highest. The results varied a bit with the precise criter but there was no great difference whether this was mental heal overall adjustment, or simply perseverance.

With a later group, Bier's more recent version of the MMPI special seminary norms, and the criterion of perseverance, some of these unfavorable patterns were confirmed. In regard to Scale 4, when it is at least the second highest, the chance of perseverance are about fifty-fifty; when it is first, they are only a little better than one in three; when it reaches or exceeds 70, they are one in three or a bit worse. When Scale 9 is paired with 4 in the highest two positions, the indication is unfavorable, but 9 does not add much to what is known from 4 alone. Other unfavorable patterns were: Scale 2 (D) highest and 0 (Si) second, 6 (Pa) highest and 3 (Hy) second. The results of the earlier study were not confirmed in regard to the combinations of 4 and 8, and those involving Scale 5. Removing this last scale from the picture is probably due to the special norms.

Some favorable profiles also emerged: Scales 2, 3, and 6 as highest; 2, 7 (Pt) and 8 as lowest; 3 highest and 6 next; 6 highest and 2 lowest; 2 highest and 9 lowest. The peculiar position of Scale 2 is to be noted.

The novices have their highest means in Mf, Pd, and Sc. Further, these and also Ma are the commonest peaks in their profiles. However, this information is based on the earlier study and cannot be checked with later data because of the change in norms.

The fact that Pd is very frequently high raises questions. There is some evidence that people who score high tend to have trouble with observing religious rules and regulations.

K is also high, on the average. Some of the data suggest a curvilinear relation to adjustment and perseverance; some, a linear. At any rate, very low scores, i.e., below a raw score of 10, suggest poor adjustment and lack of perseverance. The SD Scale (Social Desirability) is not in itself very closely related to adjustment and hardly at all to perseverance, but a combination of low SD and low K is unfavorable.

The A Scale (Anxiety) is inversely related to perseverance; R (Repression) is unrelated. However, there is a possibility that high R may act as a moderating influence.

In addition to the consideration of Ma in the profile studies, a check was made on its predictive value when taken alone. The results were not consistent, except that lower scores, i.e., less than a $\underline{T}$ of 40, seem to be associated with perseverance.

Se, which was prepared specifically to predict success in the seminary, did not survive an attempt at cross-validation; in fact, it worked a bit in the opposite direction from that intended. Wa (Work Attitude), tried because of its possible connection with motivation, was not very promising for our purposes.

Notes

1 There are two coding systems in common use, Hathaway's and Welsh's. The latter's system was used here and in the research involving all but the first classes of novices.

The clinically significant scales, Hypochondriasis (Hs) to Social Introversion (Si), are numbered from left to right in the standard profile form: Hs being 1; D, 2; . . . Ma, 9; Si, 0. Then one lists the scales in order of magnitude, using their code numbers in place of the names. The approximate size of the scores is indicated by symbols between the numbers. Any scores that differ by only one point are underlined. Ties, in the writer's modification, are indicated by a small arc (⌒) over the adjacent scale numbers. There is also a convention for listing the ? (no. of omitted items), L, F, and K scores; but this is not pertinent to the present research. A coded profile may look like this: 94'78-3650/12. Scale 9 is highest, Scale 4 is second; the prime sign (') indicates that both are 70 $\underline{T}$ score points or higher. This symbol will be referred to later. The other such symbols may be ignored, since they will not be mentioned again.

For further information, cf. Dahlstrom and Welsh, pp. 19-25. Hathaway's method will be described later, Footnote 2, and can also be found in the above reference.

2 Hathaway was the first to propose a coding method for grouping profiles according to pattern. In a sense it is simpler than Welsh's (cf. Footnote 1). The principle is essentially the same. The scales are listed by their code numbers from highest down to a $\underline{T}$ score value of 55. Scales between this value and 45 are omitted and a dash (--) is written in place of

them. Those which are 45 or lower are then put down, but now the *lowest* one comes first. If no scale is as high as 55, the profile code begins with a dash. There was one such in the group, and it is indicated in the tables by "--." The prime symbol (') is also used by Hathaway. No reference is made to Scale 0 (Si) in this section because it was not scored in the tests of this group of candidates.

A profile may read: 4'56--23. In this case, Scale 4 is highest and 70 or above; Scales 5 and 6 are next; Scale 2 is lowest and 3 next lowest; the remaining scales are in the average range, i.e., 46-54.

For further details, see Dahlstrom and Welsh, pp. 19-25.

References

Applezweig, Mortimer H.   Educational levels and Minnesota Mult phasic profiles. *J. clin. Psychol.*, 1953, 9, 340-44.

Barry, William A., S.J.   An MMPI scale for seminary candidates Unpublished Master's thesis, Fordham University, 1960.

Bier, William C., S.J.   A comparative study of a seminary grou and four other groups on the Minnesota Multiphasic Personali Inventory. *Stud. Psychol. & Psychiat., Catholic U.*, 1948, No. 3.

Brown, Hugh S.   Similarities and differences in college populations on the Multiphasic. *J. appl. Psychol.*, 1948, 32, 54 49.

Coelho, Victor Anthony, S.J.   A personality scale for candida to the priesthood. Unpublished Master's thesis, University Detroit, 1963.

Dahlstrom, W. Grant, and Welsh, George S. *An MMPI Handbook: Guide to Use in Clinical Practice and Research.* Minneapolis University of Minnesota Press, 1960.

Edwards, Allen L. *The Social Desirability Variable in Person ity Assessment and Research.* New York: Dryden, 1957.

Hathaway, S. R., and McKinley, J. C.   A multiphasic personali schedule (Minnesota): III. The measurement of symptomatic d pression. *J. Psychol.*, 1942, 14, 73-84.

McKinley, J. C., and Hathaway, S. R.   A multiphasic personali schedule (Minnesota): II. A differential study of hypochond asis. *J. Psychol.*, 1940, 10, 255-68. IV. Psychasthenia. *J. appl. Psychol.*, 1942, 26, 614-24. V. Hysteria, hypomania an psychopathic deviate. *J. appl. Psychol.*, 1944, 28, 153-74.

Skrinkosky, Peter.   A comparative study of the standard form of the Minnesota Multiphasic Personality Inventory and a modified form of the same adapted for seminary use. Unpublished Master's thesis, Fordham University, 1952.

Tydlaska, Mary, and Mengel, Robert. A scale for measuring work attitude for the MMPI. *J. appl. Psychol.*, 1953, 37, 474-77.

Weisgerber, Charles A., S.J. Comparison of normalized and linear T scores in the MMPI. *J. clin. Psychol.*, 1965, 21, 412-15.

Weisgerber, Charles A., S.J. Survey of a psychological screening program in a clerical order. In: Arnold, Magda B., *et al. Screening Candidates for the Priesthood and Religious Life.* Chicago: Loyola University Press, 1962, pp. 107-48.

Welsh, George S. Factor dimensions A and R. In: Welsh, George S., and Dahlstrom, W. Grant (Eds.) *Basic Readings on the MMPI in Psychology and Medicine.* Minneapolis: University of Minnesota Press, 1956, pp. 264-81.

Chapter 4

Motivational, Background, and Other Factors

THE emphasis on tests, particularly the MMPI, in the early years of this screening program has had the unfortunate side effect of obscuring some factors of importance in the evaluation of the candidates. Various aspects of personality, experience, life history, or circumstances at the time of application have been found to bear on subsequent adjustment and perseverance in the religious life. Some of these, like motivation and family relations, were recognized, but the extent of their influence was not fully grasped. The Sentence Completion Test had been providing some indications of motivation and family attitudes, but not always consistently; and caution had to be used in making inferences from the subject's responses. It was not until recently that a formal study was made of the validity of the test in this respect (cf. Chapter 6). The interview, autobiography, and comments of teachers or other raters also provided some clues; but, again, the information was frequently incomplete and not always dependable.

It was the gradual accumulation of experience, aided immeasurably by the feedback from the masters of novices, that

brought these and other factors to the fore. The following
were selected for study: motivation, family relations, scrupulosity, late application, and age. These were chosen
either because they had been stressed in the follow-up reports or because of impressions of the writer. These are
taken up in this chapter, rather than after concluding the
discussion of the various tests, in order to avoid constant
advance reference to data to be presented in later chapters.

Description of Factors

   Motivation is probably the most complex of these variables and the hardest to assess. Perhaps the major difficulty is that the candidate has a good idea of what his motivation ought to be like and is readily tempted, wittingly
or unwittingly, to give acceptable answers. Getting at the
matter in the interview poses a dilemma: if the questioning
is too direct, there is risk of suggesting the desirable re-
plies; if it is rather indirect, the account is often vague.
Even when the candidate gives forth the most altruistic
and supernatural motives one could wish, there is no assurance of the degree of conviction or intensity. Further,
such indications are restricted to the conscious level,
whereas the unconscious is undoubtedly important in this area.
The interview sometimes clears up the matter and often again
does not. Very often also--and quite understandably--the
candidate had initially been attracted to the priesthood or
the religious life through admiration for a priest or religious with whom he was associated. Later other motives super-
vened, and he finds it impossible to analyze the complex;
indeed, he has the company of the interviewer in his perplexity.
Another question which is practically impossible to answer is
the relative weight of natural as against supernatural motives.
There is nothing wrong, for example, if he wishes to use his
God-given talents to the best end possible; but is this simply
a natural ambition and the main driving force, or is it sub-
sumed under an overriding supernatural motive and merely secondary to it? And one could go on and on with similar problems.
   These difficulties suggest the need of a good test or other
procedure for assessing motivation unambiguously--except for
the gnawing suspicion that this is an impossible goal. From
the standpoint of the present research, the inadequacies in
evaluating this factor have restricted the available data
severely. For the whole group of entrants over a seven-year
period, there was reasonably sufficient information on a mere
113 subjects. This was derived either from the interview or
from the report of the master of novices; indications given
by the Sentence Completion Test, the autobiography, or the

raters' comments were not accepted because of doubt of their validity.

Four categories were used: good, questionable, poor, and inadequate information. Good motivation meant sufficiently supernatural and firm reasons for desiring the religious life; poor motivation, merely natural and selfish reasons or hesitation in embracing otherwise good motives. The category, "questionable," was used if the candidate, on being interrogated at length in the interview, gave a vague account of his motives; or if the master of novices, after conferences and observation, had his doubts. The danger, of course, was that this might mean that the doubt existed in the mind of either of the judges without solid foundation; but care was taken to avoid using this category unless the candidate's statements or behavior provided good basis for the doubt. The designation, "inadequate information," was applied to all other cases. The inadequacy was in part --or perhaps largely--due to the fact that the psychologist had not at the time been sensitive to this factor, assuming that it was covered by other examiners. Lastly, it should be noted that the researcher was particularly cautious about concluding that motivation was poor. In actual fact, this judgment was usually based on the report of the master of novices.

The second factor that had kept appearing in the reports on the novices who had left or had experienced difficulties was home life. For this it was somewhat easier to get information in the assessment process, but again the judgment of the master of novices was important for confirmation and occasionally for correction of misinformation. The following scheme of classification was used:

Poor: parents divorced or divorce pending, or
constant quarreling between parents, or
alcoholism or heavy drinking on part of one or
   both parents, or
one parent psychotic or very neurotic, or
candidate doesn't get along with one or both
   parents, or
serious resentment against one or both parents.
(Test information was not accepted unless clear,
v.g., several clear references in the Sentence
Completion Test.)

Fair: one parent very dominating or very possessive, or
more than ordinary sibling friction, or
family lacks unity, is disorganized, or shows
   little love and attention.

Good: only when positive evidence is present of normal
relations, v.g., unity, closeness, family loyalty,
reasonable discipline, and the like.

Inadequate information: records not clear enough to
provide a basis of judgment.

As with motivation, a large proportion of the group had to
be placed in the last category because the necessary information had not been obtained or recorded.
Scrupulosity was of particular interest to the writer
because he had made some mistakes in the early years of his
work by not giving it adequate attention. The following
classification was used:

Scrupulous: definitely is or was scrupulous for an appreciable period (more than just a few months).
Doubtful: seems scrupulous according to candidate's account but matter is not clear.
Scrupulous tendency: tendency to have an anxious conscience seen in history, i.e., short bouts of
anxiety about matters of conscience.
Inadequate information: no indication for or against
scrupulosity in record.

A fifth class, "not scrupulous," was planned but not used
because only once was the record clear enough to make this
judgment.
The remaining factors considered were late application
and age. Since the date of entrance for these novices had
been in August or September, application in July was considered late; in August or early September, very late. The
date on which the tests were administered was taken as the
time of effective application. Age was reckoned as of August
31 in the year of entry. Only the years, not the additional
months, were recorded; for example, a man was put down as
18 if he had reached his 18th birthday but not his 19th.

Subjects and Procedure

The groups chosen for study were the classes of 1956–
1962. The follow-up interval was approximately 9 1/2 years
for the first class and 3 1/2 for the last. However, the
calculations for age were made a year earlier than the rest
and were not corrected because the additional labor did not
appear worthwhile. There were originally 413 subjects. For
one, who had not been examined by the psychologist, the age
was not on record. Another 11 were excluded because the
reason for leaving the seminary was a lack of academic
ability or was unknown to the writer at the time of this
study. Only 24 had applied late and 10 very late. For the
other factors, the numbers on whom there was adequate information were: for motivation, 113; family life, 139; scru-
polosity, 34. Originally, the plan was to use the first four

classes for the pilot study and the remaining three for cross-validation, but the numbers of cases were too small for this.

Except for a passing reference later, the criterion used in the data to be reported here was solely perseverance. Overall adjustment as of the end of the novitiate was also studied, but the results added little to those obtained with the perseverance criterion.

Results

The data are shown in Tables 4.1 to 4.5. Aside from the exclusions mentioned above, the percentage of those who persevered is 57.96 and, of those who left, 42.04. These may be considered the base rate to which the other percentages may be compared.

Table 4.1

Relation of Motivation to Perseverance

| *Motivation* | Numbers | | | Percentages | |
	P	L	*Total*	P	L
Good	38	39	77	49.4	50.6
Doubtful	2	11	13	15.4	84.6
Poor	1	22	23	4.3	95.7
Total	41	72	113	36.3	63.7

Summary Statistics: $\underline{C}$ = .397; γ = .820; χ^2 = 17.852; d.f. = 1; $\underline{P}$ = .001. (Chi square computed from 2 x 2 table.

Table 4.2

Relation of Home Life to Perseverance

| *Home Life* | Numbers | | | Percentages | |
	P	L	*Total*	P	L
Good	34	36	70	48.6	51.4
Fair	11	14	25	44.0	56.0
Poor	15	29	44	34.1	65.9
Total	60	79	139	43.2	56.8

Summary Statistics: $\underline{C}$ = .129; γ = .217; χ^2 = 2.330; d.f. = 2; $\underline{P}$ = $>$ .30 (Chi square computed from 3 x 2 table.)

It is clear from Tables 4.1 and 4.2 that the subjects for whom we have adequate information about motivation and home life are not sufficiently representative of the entire group, since there is marked discrepancy of their total perseverance-percentages from that of the entire group: 36.3 in Table 4.1 and 43.2 in Table 4.2. The reason for this is not clear. Very often the information used in making the classification was derived from the report of the master of novices; in the case of those who left, he may have been more inclined to mention these things, particularly since he had been asked to give the reasons for leaving. Further, in one class there were heavy "casualities" due to a peculiar morale problem, and this fact may have distorted the picture, at least in regard to motivation. For example, without these people, the "good motivation" group would have shown 36 persevering (54.6 per cent) and 30 leaving (45.4 per cent). Even so, this is not quite as it should be, since this group ought, in view of the data for the other motivation categories, to show a better survival rate.

It is clear from Table 4.2 that motivation is very important for perseverance, perhaps the most important qualification. It will be noted that the negative side of the coin is the more significant: poor or questionable motivation is a surer indication of a poor risk than is good motivation, of a good risk. This is a phenomenon with which we are already quite familiar. Nor will this come as a surprise to anyone acquainted with the religious life, since motivation can decline as the novice loses his first enthusiasm and begins to feel the strain of a highly regulated and restricted style of living. On the other hand, if there is poor motivation to begin with, the novice is hardly prepared to meet the challenge. The findings point up the need to look most thoroughly into the reasons why the young man desires to enter the religious life. The vocation director or admissions examiner would do well to assure himself that they are adequate or to counsel the applicant until sound motivation is built up. Otherwise he risks at least a waste of time on everyone's part or possibly the loss of what might have become with less haste a solid vocation.

Of those with poor family relations, about 66 per cent leave. To these may be added those who stay but experience adjustment difficulties: an additional 7 per cent, for a total of 73 (not shown in Table 4.2). The precise nature of this influence is not always clear, since a number of quite disparate situations are included in the general rubric of "poor home life": conditions as different as breakup of the home by divorce and serious resentment toward the parents, which may be largely the fault of the candidate. In some instances it is easy to see the connection between home trouble and trouble in the novitiate, for example, when a hostile attitude to the father has been transferred to all authority figures; in other cases the reason is not readily apparent, for example, when a psychotic break in a parent occurs late enough in the life of the son for him to understand and assimilate the situation. But it does not seem to matter what the precise connection is; the outcome is the same. Probably what needs to be weighed in these cases is the attitude of the candidate: how rational is it? does it admit of forgiveness to an offending parent? does it generalize unfavorably to other authority figures? does it entail neurotic guilt feelings and a destruction of sense of personal worth? etc. Since a third of these disadvantaged novices weather the storm sufficiently to persevere, it would be unwise to exclude everyone who has had serious home problems; however, caution is necessary.

The statistics may be a little misleading in suggesting that this factor is considerably less important than motivation. From the standpoint of the subjective suffering of the novice, whether he leaves or perseveres, it may well be more important. Experience, which can be supported by case studies but not as readily by statistics, seems to indicate that poor home life, psychologically crippling as it so often is, can lead to accentuated distress in the novitiate, so that the man may leave considerably worse off than when he entered. This should certainly give us pause.

Scrupulosity is also an unfavorable condition (cf. Table 4.3). About two-thirds of those who are or have been scru-

Table 4.3

Relation of Scrupulosity to Perseverance

Condition	Numbers			Percentages	
	P	L	Total	P	L
Scrupulous	8	17	25	32.0	68.0
Doubtful	3	1	4	75.0	25.0
Scrup. Tendency	4	1	5	80.0	20.0
Total	15	19	34	44.1	55.9

pulous fail to persevere. When there is some doubt about the matter or merely a tendency to scrupulosity, the attrition rates are ostensibly quite low, 25 and 20 per cent respectively. However, the subgroups together totalled only 9 cases. With later data and a total of 18, the percentage was 44 (cf. Chapter 5, Table 5.3). This is more plausible

but still below the base rate. Yet the problem of unreliability of data from a small sample remains. Or perhaps these
findings should suggest caution in judging the presence of
scrupulosity. However, no one of any experience with religious
would deny that the picture presented by the data on the active-
ly scrupulous is essentially correct. Nor is it necessary to
explain why scrupulosity is an unfavorable condition.

Late application, as may be seen in Table 4.4, does not

Table 4.4

Relation of Late Application to Perseverance

| | Numbers | | | Percentages | |
	P	L	Total	P	L
Late	7	17	24	29.2	70.8
Very Late	4	6	10	40.0	60.0
Total	11	23	34	32.4	67.6

make for perseverance. However, there is an oddity in the
data, since the very late do better than the late. The only
reasonable explanation that comes to mind is that the numbers involved are quite small and data derived from small
samples are notoriously unreliable. If one more of the very
late applicants should leave, the percentages would be quite
in line. In some instances late application is due to such
circumstances as delays in correspondence, attendance at
distant boarding schools, and so on. However, it is more often
symptomatic of indecision, which was finally terminated by
an impulsive decision as the beginning of the new school year
approached. Either the initial indecision or the final impulsive decision is probably the significant condition. And
further risk is created by the pressure on the examiners to
explore and evaluate in haste.

Questions are often asked regarding the attrition rate
among older candidates; hence the inclusion of this variable
in the study. It is clear from Table 4.5 that age generally
has no significant effect on perseverance; the various figures for the two groups are practically identical.

So far these conditions have been considered independently of one another. To what extent do they have a cumulative effect: v.g., what happens if both motivation and
home life are poor? An attempt was made to answer this question, but the number of such cases was too small; in fact,
there were only five.

Table 4.5

Age and Perseverance

	Persevered	*Left*
Mean	19.13	19.03
Median	18.13	18.12
Mode	18.00	18.00
S.D.	2.70	2.74
Range	16-32	17-40
Modified Range*	17-23	17-22

*I.e., 10th to 90th percentiles.

The reader will note that $\underline{C}$, γ , and χ^2 are given only
for motivation and family relations. They are not appropriate
for the other tables. In regard to motivation, the figures
confirm the impression of an appreciable relation to perseverance. Family background, on the other hand, seems to be
only slightly associated with this criterion. In both cases,
however, the full story is told only by the data in the
tables themselves: it is the unfavorable end of the continuum
that is of significance. But this has been discussed previously. Biserial correlation might have been used with the data
on age, but it is obvious that it would be practically zero.

Whether we are explicitly aware of it or not, we commonly base our predictions for the future on our experiences
of the past. In assessing candidates, we assume that future
classes will be much like those examined in previous years.
While there is some risk in this assumption, it is better
than a purely *a priori* approach. The percentages given in
the tables may be treated as probability estimates: i.e.,
if some 96 per cent of the poorly motivated have left the
religious life, we judge that there are about 96 chances in
100 that a poorly motivated candidate will leave, and hence
we consider him an exceedingly poor risk.

In order to summarize the relation of the definitely unfavorable indicators, Table 4.6 has been drawn up. These indicators are more effective than all or almost all of those
previously derived from the MMPI. Poor motivation especially
is a powerful predictor. The thought that suggests itself
is to devise some system in which these factors are given
due weight, much after the manner of actuarial prediction
used successfully by insurance companies. Such a system
has, in fact, been developed and applied tentatively to
recent classes. The results will be presented later
(cf. Chapter 9).

Table 4.6

Summary of Unfavorable Factors

	Left
Motivation poor or doubtful	91.7%
Family relations poor	65.9
Scrupulous	68.0
Late or very late application	70.8
Base rate	42.0

Conclusions

To present the conclusions in summary form—poor or questionable motivation, poor family relations, scrupulosity, and late application do not augur well for perseverance in the religious life. This is most striking in respect of motivation. It is necessary, therefore, to give these factors close attention in the assessing of candidates, whether by tests or other means.

If there is serious question regarding the motives of an applicant, he ought hardly ever to be accepted at the time. Further counseling and spiritual direction would give him a chance to clarify and develop his goals. An adequate test of motivation is highly desirable.

Age has nothing to do with perseverance generally. This, however, is not to deny that it may have relevance in some cases.

Chapter 5

Time Aspects

THIS chapter concerns two questions: what are the characteristics of those who leave the novitiate after a very short time? and is long-term prediction possible? Although the two questions are somewhat disparate in their intent, they are grouped together because they both have to do with the lapse of time between entry and the application of a criterion.

Those Who Leave Early

One of the most frustrating aspects of vocational work, whether promotion, guidance, or screening, is the phenomenon of the candidate who goes through all of the preparation for entering the novitiate and then leaves very shortly, before he has had a chance really to understand the life or to profit either himself or the order. One is at a loss to imagine what could possibly have gone through his mind to make him take such a serious step and then to back away so soon. Clearly he has wasted a good bit of time for himself and

everyone involved. Accordingly, a study was undertaken to
see whether there are any characteristics which might
serve to identify these candidates in advance.

For convenience of expression we shall call these men
"early leavers." In this religious order there are certain
critical stages that occur early in the novitiate, and it
would be good if we could analyze the data according to
these stages. For example, there is a period of instruction
and reflection for about twelve days preceding formal admission to the novitiate. But even over a number of years
there are so few cases of departure during this period that
it is impossible to gain anything by such a fine breakdown of the data. Hence, we shall take the first three
months after entry and consider all those who leave within
this period as early leavers. The choice of three months
rather than four or five is somewhat arbitrary, but it is
only a fourth of a year and is short enough so that the
novice has not really given the life an adequate test.

The subjects studied were the members of the classes of
1956–1965. For the investigation of some of the variables,
earlier groups could have been included; but the MMPI scores
were not comparable because of the change to Bier's 1955
revision. To keep the pool of subjects constant for the
various aspects of the study, no attempt was made to dip
into the earlier group. It should be remarked that in a few
cases there was some doubt whether an individual might have
stayed a little beyond three months, but these were put in
the group of early leavers because the exact determination
of the date did not seem critical.

The background factors considered were those discussed
in Chapter 4, except for the omission of age. The MMPI characteristics were: the high point in the profile and a few
combinations. The range of profile types which could profit-
ably be investigated was rather limited because of the familiar difficulty of the small number of cases in the subgroups. For example, there were 55 who had their highest
score on Scale 4 (Pd). When this group was subdivided and
only those were counted who showed a T score of 70 or more,
there were only 14.

Results

The data are presented in Tables 5.1 to 5.3. The column
labelled N gives the number of cases showing the particular
characteristic, and the percentages are based on this number
as divisor. In the second-last column of each table the heading says, "2nd Yr." This is not a completely accurate designation. On occasion, a novice is not admitted to vows at the
normal time but is deferred for six months or, more rarely,

Table 5.1

Relation of High Point of MMPI Profile to Time of Leaving

High Point	N**	3 Mos.	Left Within* 1st Yr.	2nd Yr.	Lat
1	41	12.2%	24.4%	34.1%	53.
2	52	7.7	11.5	30.8	50.
3	67	9.0	19.4	31.3	43.
4	55	10.9	34.5	50.9	69.
5	57	10.5	28.1	36.8	47.
6	60	8.3	21.7	30.0	50.
7	28	10.7	32.1	50.0	60.
8	32	9.4	21.9	40.6	59.
9	71	8.5	26.8	36.6	57.
0	55	3.6	20.0	40.0	50.
Ties***	44	18.2	27.3	40.9	56.
Total****	585	9.6	23.4	36.8	54.

    * The figures below are cumulative.
    ** N is the number of those with the given high point.
    *** That is, two or more scales were tied for highest.
    **** These totals include a few men who had not taken the
test, had used the wrong form of it, and the like.

Table 5.2

Other MMPI Profile Features and Time of Leaving

Feature	N	3 Mos.	Left Within 1st Yr.	2nd Yr.	Lat
4' (and 1st or tied for 1st)	14	21.4%	50.0%	50.0%	57.
4' (not necessarily 1st)	25	20.0	40.0	48.0	64.
4 in 1st two (incl. ties for 2nd)	122	11.5	27.0	42.6	63.
49, 49, or 94	26	11.5	26.9	38.5	53.
9' (not necessarily 1st)	23	13.0	30.4	47.8	69.
9 in 1st two (incl. ties for 2nd)	142	9.9	26.8	38.7	60.

Table 5.3

Background Factors and Time of Leaving

Factor	N	3 Mos.	Left Within 1st Yr.	2nd Yr.	Later
Motivation:					
Poor or Doubtful	63	33.7%	63.5%	77.8%	85.7%
Good	136	6.6	22.1	34.6	57.4
Application:					
Late	29	20.7	41.4	58.6	75.9
Very Late	10	20.0	40.0	60.0	60.0
Family Relations:					
Poor	76	14.5	31.6	51.3	71.1
Fair	51	17.6	37.3	52.9	68.6
Good	103	9.7	22.3	35.0	60.2
Scrupulosity:					
Scrupulous	48	22.9	31.2	47.9	66.7
Doubtful or tendency*	18	11.1	11.1	27.8	44.4

* That is, seemed scrupulous, but matter was not clear; or had a tendency to be scrupulous.

longer. These cases are included in the "2nd Yr." group because it appears more meaningful to place together all who failed to reach the point of taking vows. The percentages given in the very last line (or row) yield an estimate of the base rate, since they show the percentages of the entire group who left, regardless of MMPI profile. The other percentages must be measured against these in order to determine whether they signify a greater or less incidence of leaving. A similar function is served by the column headed "Later," which permits us to compare the indications of early leaving as against simply leaving at some time or other. Like the percentages in the two preceding columns, these are cumulative: i.e., they include those who had left previously.

One general impression yielded by the tables is that the factors associated with early leaving are, with few exceptions, the same as those associated with leaving at any time. Or, to put it more simply, there is little difference between those who leave early and those who leave later.

As to those who do not last beyond three months, the important factors are: poor or doubtful motivation, scrupulosity, late application, poor or questionable family relations, a notably high score (T of 70 or above) on Scale

4 (Pd). There are few changes as we go on then to the end of the first year. The importance of motivation stands out more strikingly. And so also for family relations. The role of Scale 4 is further apparent; particularly, it now becomes clear that having this as the highest scale is a liability, even if it does not reach the level of 70 $\underline{T}$ score units. Scale 9 (Ma), if 70 or higher, is also an unfavorable indicator.

The data for the whole of the first year and for the second have been included in the tables, despite our original definition of "early" as meaning the first three months, because they help to clarify the picture. Some of the unfavorable characteristics have been brought out more clearly.

One feature of the data in Table 5.1 is the matter of ties, i.e., of instances in which two or more MMPI scales are tied for the highest. Defections in this group are rather frequent in the first three months. Any or all of scales may be involved in these ties, so that it is impossible to look to their psychological meaning for suggestions of the reason. Nor is the group large enough to make it worthwhile to sub-classify according to the precise scales which are tied. The most readily intelligible would be ties of Scales 4 and 9, but there was only one such case in this sample. For the present we must apparently do without an explanation.

From the standpoint of identifying in advance those who are likely to leave the novitiate early, the indicators are not as helpful as one might wish. The clearest of them, poor or doubtful motivation, shows an early-mortality rate of only 33.3 per cent. On the other hand, 78 per cent leave in the novitiate and about 90 per cent do so eventually. (The figure is 92 in Table 4.6 and 86 per cent for the present sample.) All things considered, the loss of one-third in the first three months gives added weight to the suggestion made in the preceding chapter that such candidates should be told to wait until there is some assurance that they have developed adequate motives. The only other factors that we can seriously consider are late application and a $\underline{T}$ score of 70 or above on Scale 4 of the MMPI. The early-leaving rates for these are about 20 per cent, but by the end of the novitiate the figure is roughly 50–60. This is high, but no one engaged in vocation work would be willing to sacrifice the remaining 40 or 50 per cent who are good prospects. Hence, while we should be cautious in evaluating these people, we should generally n exclude them, unless there are other reasons for so doing.

Conclusions

1 It is not really possible, with the present information, to identify specifically those who will leave the religious life very early. The factors associated with early leaving are much the same as those associated with leaving at any time.

2 Poor or doubtful motivation, however, indicates with a high degree of probability those who will leave eventually, if not early, and may be used as indication of such a poor risk that postponement of admission seems advisable.

3 Late application or a score of at least 70 on Scale 4 of the MMPI suggests caution but not rejection or deferral of the candidate.

Short- vs. Long-Term Prediction

In efforts at screening candidates for the priesthood and religious orders, it has apparently been assumed at least implicitly that a long-range prediction of psychological fitness is possible at the time of application. The psychologist's assigned task has been not merely to eliminate the few who are obviously unfit here and now, but more particularly those who have pathological tendencies which make them poor risks for the indefinite future. This is quite a feat if it can be done. The purpose of this section is to present some evidence on this point.

Method

The data have been taken from the records of 200 men admitted to the novitiate in 1950-1954 and 352, in 1956-1961. All those who entered in these years have been included, except a few whose records were for some reason incomplete and one who could not be followed up. Those required to leave because of academic failure or advised to leave because of poor health are included in the original count but excluded at the appropriate point: i.e., in the tabulations for the year in which they left the order. This will be explained more fully later. The members of the 1950 class had completed seventeen and three-fourths years in the religious life at the date of this study; the 1961 class, six and three-fourths years. The criterion used was perseverance vs. dropping out. With such a long span of time, it would have been quite difficult to obtain ratings on all subjects at each year of their progress; and since the study was conceived recently, it was in fact impossible. Although this criterion is not of a piece with the psychologist's judgments, which concerned mental health and personality, it has been found to yield similar results to those ob-

103

tained with ratings on mental health and adjustment (cf. Chapter 2).

The two groups of classes were studied separately because of disparity in the basis of the predictions. For the first group the judgment of fitness had generally been based on the MMPI and other written information, but a number of the men were interviewed and/or given further tests. From the 1957 class on, all had been seen by a psychologist. However, the records of the judgment after the interview were not available at the time of this analysis for one of the novitiates. Hence, the judgment based on the tests and allied material was followed rather than that after the interview. Another reason for keeping the two groups separate was the difference in length of follow-up. From this standpoint, one may question the advisability of including classes as recent as 1960 and 1961. Aside from getting a greater number of cases, the reason will be apparent later.

Results

The data for the first group are presented in Table 5.4, which gives the rate of drop-out according to years of training. The tabulation was not carried beyond year 13, the last completed by all of the classes in this group.

In computing the percentages, various approaches could have been used, but it seemed best to take as the divisor the number of seminarians in each category (satisfactory or doubtful-unsatisfactory) who were present at the beginning of the year. These are the totals listed in the table. One of these was adjusted and is indicated by underlining. One man had left because of academic failure and, since this reason does not reflect unfavorably on his mental health or personality, he was excluded. He might, of course, have simply been removed from the original total, i.e., at the beginning of the first year; however, this seemed a less accurate way of calculating the percentages for the earlier years, and might readily entail recalculations of all the data any time one wished to bring the figures up to date subsequently. Hence, the compromise was reached of excluding him from the total for the year in which he left—and, of course, subsequently. (The same procedure was followed for the later group, in which one had left for academic reasons and one because of poor health.)

The first class had completed seventeen and three-fourths years of training; the last, thirteen and three-fourths. The differences in the last column of the table provide a convenient way of comparing the drop-out rates of the two categori the percentage for the satisfactory being subtracted from tha for the doubtful and unsatisfactory.

Table 5.4

Judgment of Fitness and Drop-out Rate by Year of
   Training: 1950-1954 Classes

		Judgment			
			Doubtful or		
	Satisfactory		Unsatisfactory		
Year	Total	Left	Total	Left	Difference
1	169	13.6%	31	35.5%	21.9%
2	146	5.5	20	.0	-5.5
3	138	2.9	20	5.0	2.1
4	134	.7	19	.0	-.7
5	133	.8	19	.0	-.8
6	132	2.3	19	.0	-2.3
7	129	3.9	19	.0	-3.9
8	124	3.2	19	.0	-3.2
9	120	2.5	<u>18</u>	5.6	3.1
10	117	4.3	17	.0	-4.3
11	112	5.4	17	11.8	6.4
12	106	3.8	15	.0	-3.8
13	102	1.0	15	13.3	12.3

Note--Totals are the number who began the year. The total
underlined (18) was adjusted because one case was excluded,
since the reason for leaving was academic failure.

Appreciably more of the latter leave in the first year,
which involves adjustment to a new way of life and the considerable stress of an intensive spiritual training. For
several years after that it is more often the satisfactory
ones that leave. Later the preponderance shifts again to the
doubtful side of the ledger. This is perhaps due to the fact
that theological studies and then ordination are approaching,
which occasion a certain amount of soul-searching and are
likely to bring to the fore the personality weaknesses that
had caused concern to the psychologist initially. Further
data, of course, are needed to determine whether this trend
is more than accidental; the percentages, even when they
seem appreciable, are based on a small number of cases.
    For this reason the data for the 1956-1961 classes are
shown in Table 5.5, despite their comparative recency. The
last group were approaching the end of their seventh year,
but the analysis was stopped at the end of the sixth year.
To carry the tabulation beyond this point was a problem.
In order to get some kind of test of the change of trend

Table 5.5

Judgment of Fitness and Drop-out Rate by Year of
    Training: 1956-1961 Classes

		Judgment			
			Doubtful or		
	Satisfactory		Unsatisfactory		
Year	Total	Left	Total	Left	Differenᴄ
1	231	17.3%	121	28.1%	10.8%
2	191	12.6	87	17.2	4.6
3	167	4.8	72	2.8	-2.0
4	159	5.0	70	2.9	-2.1
5	151	4.6	68	1.5	-3.1
6	143	8.4	67	7.5	-.9
7	118	6.8	53	3.8	-3.0
8	93	7.5	41	2.4	-5.1
9	67	6.0	30	6.7	.7
10	45	2.2	18	.0	-2.2
11	16	6.2	12	25.0	18.8

    Note—Numbers underlined have the same meaning as in Table
5.4. The sixth year is the last one completed by all of the
classes. From the seventh year on, those have been excluded
who had not yet completed the year in question; hence, the
pronounced decrease in the totals.

noted at years eleven and thirteen in the previous sample, it
was desirable to retain as much data as possible for the later
years. The solution chosen was to eliminate the last class for
year seven, and then one further class per year, working back
until year eleven, in which the data are based on only one cla
This drastically reduces the totals involved in these years.
    These data tend to confirm the relations noted with the
earlier group. More of the doubtful-unsatisfactory leave in
the first year than the satisfactory; only a trifle more in
the second year; then the situation is reversed until the
eleventh year. While we are again dealing with small numbers
leaving in each of the later years and have, by our method,
cut down the totals which serve as the divisors for the percentages, still it is interesting that these data agree fairly well with the preceding and give them at least some confirmation. However, it is clear that we need to wait for
more cases before lending much credence to these results.
    At the risk of belaboring a point, another method of
analysis is used in Tables 5.6 and 5.7, which express the

Table 5.6

Relation of Judgment of Fitness to Perseverance in
Terms of $\underline{C}$ and γ : 1950-1954 Classes

Year	C	γ	χ^2	P
1	.211	.555	8.883	.01
2	.152	.420	4.639	.05
4	.148	.400	4.352	.05
6	.124	.341	3.080	.10
8	.076	.215	1.166	.30
10	.072	.201	1.031	.50
12	.075	.207	1.114	.30
13	.119	.320	2.811	.10

Table 5.7

Relation of Judgment of Fitness to Perseverance in
Terms of $\underline{C}$ and γ : 1956-1961 Classes

Year	C	γ	χ^2	P
1	.126	.302	5.561	.02
2	.130	.279	5.960	.02
4	.090	.191	2.840	.10
6	.055	.115	1.047	.40

accuracy of the psychologist's judgments in terms of statistical measures we have used previously. The years indicated in the first column are to be understood as up to
and including the end of the year, reckoned from the date
of entrance. The various figures are cumulative: that is
for example, the drop-outs at the end of the second year
include those in the first year, and so for the rest. The
statistics in Table 5.7 stop at the end of the sixth year
because of the difficulty explained previously.

The $\underline{C}$ coefficients indicate a rather slight relation
between prediction and perseverance in general, but one
which is a little better for the first year, then declines
for several years, and finally takes a turn upward (Table
5.6 only). The γ figures show essentially the same relationship. Chi square is given solely because it is the basis
for $\underline{C}$ and provides a means of obtaining the estimate of
probability.

The decrease in apparent relation between the psychologist's judgment and the criterion of perseverance was ex-

pected; the later increase was not. On the basis of some years of experience and a preliminary survey, the hypothesis had been formed that prediction by means of tests or other forms of personality assessment is impossible beyond a period of four or five years, perhaps even beyond two. The present data seem at first to fit this assumption, but the results for the later years of follow-up suggest that one cannot yet rule out the possibility of long-term prediction.

Conclusions

There is question regarding the acceptability of the criterion and the reliability of the various percentages. The latter are for the most part based on large enough total groups; but the number of men leaving in each year, after the first and second, is small. Further follow-up is also necessary. However, with these limitations in mind, one can draw some conclusions. In the first place, what success the psychologist has—and it is modest—is found primarily in the first year, with sometimes a little addition in the second, third, and fourth years. For a period of about six years after that, the record does not flatter him. However, there is some evidence, albeit not more than suggestive, in favor of prediction for a longer term (11 to 13 years in this study). One can certainly not be as sanguine about long-term prediction as some of the literature on screening of seminarians has implied. On the other hand, one cannot simply pass it off as completely impossible. *"Adhuc sub judice lis est."*

Chapter 6

Sentence Completion Test

ALTHOUGH a Sentence Completion Test has been used in this screening program since 1956, very little research effort has been devoted to it. This is partly a side-effect of the attention given to the MMPI and partly a consequence of the fact that the writer's approach to this instrument has been clinical rather than psychometric. Various scoring methods have been devised for this type of test, and some have a respectable amount of evidence in favor of their validity and usefulness. However, scoring systems tend to reduce the information to abstract, formalized measures of traits, needs, attitudes, and the like. All of this has, indeed, its value; but it may obscure the most significant contribution of the test, which is the rich, concrete indication of what the person is thinking, how he views his family, what motives and fears he gives expression to, and so on.

Method of Interpretation

The Sentence Completion Test is usually regarded as a projective technique, and projection probably is found in many of the subject's responses. Still, when and how projection enters in is difficult to determine, if not impossible. Hence, the writer's practice has been to take the statements at face value, but with appropriate reservation. Some of the information is quite straightforward. For example, such facts as divorce, desertion, death or serious illness of a parent, will usually be revealed or hinted at. On the other hand, if lack of affection or attention, unreasonable disciplinary practices, friction are asserted, the subject may not be stating objective facts; however, he is at least reflecting his own attitudes, which are important clinically. At other times, he may be projecting and excusing a bad home situation by asserting that other families have the same problem as his, or even worse. Some responses are patently honest, as for example, when the subject says that on seeing the person in charge coming he quickly looks to see if he is doing his job or gets busy. (This is so common a response that the writer takes it as evidence of honesty and normality, while he regards the denial of concern with some suspicion.)

The sentence stems are comparatively long, so that the subject's associations will be channeled in certain directions. Nevertheless, there is considerable latitude of choice. As a consequence, the test does not consistently give one the same type or amount of information. There are quite a number of characteristics which may come out quite clearly in an occasional record, but not be noted at all in the majority. A tendency to feel under the pressure of time in school work is one such factor. These are noted for further investigation in the interview, but they are not frequent enough to be susceptible to statistical treatment.

The principles of interpretation that have been used may be summarized as follows: First, the responses are taken at face value, i.e., as what the candidate is conscious of and is willing to divulge; while caution is exercised, the presumption is honesty and frankness unless indications are otherwise (in the test itself or in other sources of information). Second, attention is given to topics which are repeatedly mentioned, whether because of the nature of the sentence stems or not. Third, related responses are examined for consistency. Fourth, although statements which purportedly deal with facts may or may not be accurate, they generally reflect attitudes which are just as important as facts, if not more so. This, of course, is a principle one also applies in a clinical interview. Fifth, any expression of unusual intensity of feeling is noted. Sixth—but probably first in importance—the impressions gleaned from the test are taken as hypotheses to be checked by interview or other means. Seventh, the more a response sounds like a catechism answer or tends to the conventional and socially-acceptable, the greater the caution needed.

Generally the interpretation does not lend itself to distinction of degrees of intensity or seriousness. Thus, for example, the conclusion may be reached that the candidate has inferiority feelings, worries about his studies, may be scrupulous, and so on; but it is not possible, short of a good bit of risky inference, to tell the extent to which these problems are bothersome. Hence the reports, in as far as they are dependent on the Sentence Completion Test, merely speak of the presence or absence of such things. However, it is usually feasible to describe family relations as good, fair, or poor; and motivation as good, doubtful, or (with considerable hesitation) poor; and the reasons for these distinctions can be sufficiently specified.

Description of the Test

The Sentence Completion Test first used was obtained from Bier. It is reproduced in Appendix D. Some items, particularly those concerning sex, occasioned complaint on the score that the candidates were being asked to write down confessional matter and had no idea who might see their answers. Although this claim seemed exaggerated, for best results one desires a favorable attitude to the test; hence, these items were dropped and the candidates were instructed to use code numbers in place of their names. Actually, the sentences dealing with sex rarely provided any information beyond the fact that the subjects knew their catechism lessons. At the same time, some other items were dropped because they yielded little material and a few substitutions were made. The test was also shortened so that it would ordinarily require no more than 45 minutes to complete, even with men who work slowly or lack fluency. The revised version is reproduced here.

SENTENCE COMPLETION TEST

Code No. _____   Date _____

This test allows you to express your feelings, attitudes, and ambitions about various topics. Some items may strike you as a little personal; some may be a little hard to complete because they don't seem to apply to you. Feel free to omit such items but do not omit more than five all told.

The sentences may be as long or short as you wish, but in most cases you will write more than a word or two. Please do not try to be humorous. There is no time limit, but you should finish in 30 to 45 minutes. Don't spend too much time on any one item.

1 I feel that a real friend _____
2 When the odds are against me _____
3 I would like to forget the time I _____
4 If I were in charge _____
5 To me the future looks _____
6 My superiors _____
7 I wish I weren't, but I am afraid of _____
8 My father hardly ever _____
9 When I was a child _____
10 My ideal of a woman is _____
11 My feeling about married life is _____
12 Most of all I want to _____
13 Compared with most families, mine _____
14 I don't like people who _____
15 My mother _____
16 I believe that I have the ability to _____
17 My greatest mistake was _____
18 In my school, my teachers _____
19 At times I feel _____
20 If my father would only _____
21 I was never happier than _____
22 I think most girls _____
23 My fellow students _____
24 I worry _____
25 Most families I know _____
26 I think a wife should _____
27 If I could only _____
28 My mother and I _____
29 The people I like best _____
30 My greatest weakness is _____
31 Some day I _____
32 When I see the person in charge coming _____
33 At times I have felt ashamed _____
34 Compared with my mother, my dad _____
35 My most vivid childhood memory _____
36 What I like least about women _____
37 My family treats me like _____
38 I like working with people who _____
39 My mother thinks that my father _____
40 When I am not around, my friends _____
41 Compared with others, I _____
42 I look forward to _____
43 My fears sometimes force me to _____
44 My father and I _____
45 I remember when _____

```
46  When I think of women _____
47  When I was a child, my family _____
48  I feel that sex is _____
49  People who work with me usually _____
50  What I want out of life _____
```

The remaining space may be used to comment on one or
more of the sentences, if you wish.

(Space allowed here.)

The reliability of the test has not been investigated by
the writer. Some of the usual methods of evaluation are excluded because of the nature of projective techniques. There
are cases in the files in which the test was repeated after
a year, but they are too few to make use of the test-retest
method. A possible approach that suggests itself is to compare interpretations of two or more psychologists. However,
in the routine use of the test it has been necessary to
write comments on the protocols, and this would effectively
destroy the independence of the evaluations. Furthermore,
unless a formal scoring method is applied to the whole test,
the best one could do would be to use some figure like the
percentage of agreement on a few things like family relations
and motivation. Hence, we must confess that the reliability
of the test is unknown.

The previous remarks about the variations in kinds of information yielded suggest that we shall be unable even to approach a thorough study of validity. After a little experience, it becomes quite obvious that some characteristics cannot be judged validly. For example, pride is often mentioned
as the subject's greatest weakness. Anyone familiar with
Catholic education and training will see in this admission
the reflection of religious instruction, a sermon, a retreat,
or spiritual direction; in fact, the admission is in itself
a reason for doubt that the failing is present to a significant degree. It is also clear that some sentence stems
very frequently evoke stereotyped remarks, for example,
"What I like least about women is that they talk too much."
Such responses are of no value.

Some evidence, nevertheless, can be presented regarding
the test's validity. As has previously been indicated, one
always gets some information regarding family relations and
motivation. Since it has been shown in Chapter 4 that these
factors are extremely important for perseverance in the religious life, they have been chosen for study.

The subjects selected were those who applied to one novitiate in 1960-1964. By this time most of the copies of the

113

older form of the test had been exhausted, so that the revised form was used with all but a few. However, except when
a scoring method was finally tried for the motivation factor, the change of form posed no problem, since both give
sufficient scope to expression of family relations and motivation.

Family Relations

The judgment as to family relations had often been written
on the test protocol or equivalent notations had been made;
when this was not the case, the writer reexamined the protocol
and made the judgment. This was done without knowledge of the
criterion, i.e., the writer did not consult his other notes
and did not recall what they had indicated. He was, however,
somewhat aware of the candidate's later record. The basis of
the criterion judgment varied. In most instances it was expressed in the report to the superior after the psychological
interview, or it was noted down in the candidate's file. In
many cases, it was a report from the master of novices. It
is hard to say to what extent the criterion judgment was independent of the Sentence Completion Test. The interview is
guided by all the information contained in this test, the
MMPI, the autobiography, the comments of those who fill out
the recommendation forms, and a summary of the observations
of others who have examined the man. If the sentence completions suggest a family problem, this area is explored in
greater detail. The writer keeps his files as brief as possible and generally does not repeat in his permanent notes
things that he has included in his report. As a consequence
it was frequently impossible to determine why he had, for
example, come to the conclusion that family relations were
good. However, he has constantly avoided basing his final
judgment on the tests alone. Hence, it is reasonably sure
that the criterion reflects more than just his consistency,
although it is certainly contaminated to some extent.
    For both judgments, that based on the test and that used
as the criterion, family relations were classified as good,
fair, or poor. A fourth category, "inadequate information,"
was added for the criterion array. The reason for the difference in treatment is this: The test provides so many
occasions for saying something positive or negative about
the family that failure to do so was taken to suggest eva-
sion and hence to give some reason for doubt. The occasional such doubtful case was put in the "fair" category. However, in regard to the criterion judgment, a stricter approach seemed called for. Sometimes inadequate information
was not due to a lack of facts, but rather to doubt about

114

their interpretation. In some instances it was simply the result of oversight in taking notes or making the report, so that neither facts nor interpretation had been recorded.

In determining which of the classes applied to a given case, two procedures were used, in accordance with the information already available. (1) When family relations had already been classified as good, fair, or poor in the comments written on the test protocol by the author, this judgment was followed. An alternate strategy could have been adopted, with perhaps greater fairness to the tests: that of ignoring previous judgments and making the classifications afresh. Still, it was argued that this would result in correcting some of the writer's previous mistakes, and that these mistakes should be let stand if one wants a realistic picture of how the instrument has worked out in practice. (2) When the protocol did not contain such a notation, then the judgment was made at the time of this study, according to specified norms. These norms were the same as those indicated in Chapter 4 (cf. p. 90).

This dual procedure has been described, for the sake of convenience, with reference to the Sentence Completion Test. It applies also to the criterion judgment, *mutatis mutandis*. In place of "comments on the test protocol" read "psychological report or the writer's notes." The basic information often came ultimately from the master of novices--and happily so from the research standpoint.

The number of cases is 146 for family relations, after the exclusion of 15 because of inadequate criterion information.

Results

The test judgments were cross-tabulated against the criterion judgments in the usual manner; the results are presented in Table 6.1. The main part of this table gives the frequencies. The numbers underlined represent the cases of direct confirmation of the test results; they total 91 for a percentage of 62.4, which is neither very high nor a great improvement over the base rate, 53.4 per cent. However, Cramér's $\underline{C}$ is .415. Although this statistic is not directly comparable to Pearson's product-moment correlation nor translatable (as for example ϕ) into an estimate of the equivalent $\underline{r}$, it suggest a degree of relationship which is similar to that often found when aptitude tests are correlated with performance criteria. The γ coefficient of .720 is good, indicating a marked tendency for the test to align the subjects in the same order as that on the criterion. To bring out more clearly the predictive value of the test for the group rated "poor" according to it, Chi square was

Table 6.1

Sentence Completion Test: Identification of Family Relations

Criterion Information

Test	Good	Fair	Poor	Total	Per Cent Good
Good	<u>61</u>	9	6	76	80.3
Fair	11	<u>12</u>	15	38	28.9
Poor	6	8	<u>18</u>	32	18.8
Total	78	29	39	146	53.4

Summary Statistics: Correct: 91 = 62.4%; $\underline{C}$ = .415; γ = .720; χ^2 = 50.230; d.f. = 4; $\underline{P}$ = .001.

re-computed from a 3 x 2 table, by combining the "Fair" and "Poor" columns. This compression also meets the objection that the theoretical frequencies in three cells of the original table are close to the minimally acceptable size. The figure was 46.628, significant at the .001 level. According to this evidence, then, the test has some validity.

The last column of the table presents, for each of the classes according to the test, the percentage who actually enjoyed a good family life. These show a progression from 18.8 for the "Poor" to 80.3 for the "Good" group, and thus offer some confirmation of the other summary statistics. But they are mainly of interest in regard to determining where accuracy is greatest and where it is poorest. The extremes, both good and poor family relations, are identified with 80 per cent accuracy, which is rather good for personality tests. It is in the middle category ("Fair") that the major source of error lies. This is especially clear if we look at the frequencies in the body of the table and note that less than one-third (12/38) of these ratings were correct.

Validity may also be gauged against the criterion of perseverance. Data on this are presented in Table 6.2. The total number of cases is smaller because it includes, of course, only those who entered the novitiate. The data are not as orderly as in the preceding table. Both $\underline{C}$ and γ are .280, although χ^2, which is 9.960, reaches the .01 level of significance. There is an association between the test results and perseverance, but it is in general not very strong. On the other hand, the situation is quite different for those labelled "poor" according to the test; only three (13.6 per cent) persevered. This is in keeping with the findings

Table 6.2

Sentence Completion Test: Family Relations and Perseverance

Family Relations	Persevered	Left	Total	Per Cent Persevered
Good	34	38	72	47.2
Fair	18	15	33	54.6
Poor	3	19	22	13.6
Total	55	72	127	43.3

Summary Statistics: $\underline{C}$ = .280; γ = .280; χ^2 = 9.960; d.f. = 2; $\underline{P}$ = .01.

reported in Chapter 4. Nor is it unusual for a test to give better results in terms of some "performance" criterion at the bottom end of its range.

Motivation

The Sentence Completion Test also offers some indications of the motivation of the subject. One is interested in two aspects, the kinds of motives that have guided him and the intensity of his desire to become a religious. The judgment is not as easy to make as in the case of home life. What one looks for particularly are expressions of supernatural and altruistic motives. The sentence stems which tend to elicit such expressions do not compel the testee to relate them to the religious life; one naturally infers this relation but risks error in doing so.

Motivation, according to the test protocols, was classified as good, doubtful, or poor. It was considered good if it was supernatural in any way. The degree of confidence in this judgment varied; particularly was it hesitant when there was one such mention as against several of natural and self-centered goals, or when the responses indicated a feeling of obligation to enter the religious life. The judgment of "doubtful" meant that the protocol gave too little information or suggested unsatisfactory motives, but not clearly enough to justify a harsher verdict. The "poor" rating was used when there was positive mention of self-centered motives and nothing beyond these.

The information for the criterion judgment was obtained in the way and according to the norms described in Chapter 4. As in the case of family relations, there was a fourth category for inadequate information. Again, the psychologist's reports or notes were followed if they already contained a statement placing the candidate in a definite category and it was not contradicted by later information from the master of novices; otherwise the judgment was made at the time of this study.

The number of cases was 133, after the exclusion of 28 because of inadequate information regarding criterion.

Results

The results of tabulating test against criterion are to be found in Table 6.3. The number of correct identifications was 90 (67.7 per cent). Chi square could not be computed

Table 6.3

Sentence Completion Test:
   Identification of Quality of Motivation

Criterion Information

Test	*Good*	*Doubtful*	*Poor*	*Total*	Per Cent *Good*
Good	75	11	4	90	83.3
Doubtful	19	8	1	28	67.9
Poor	5	2	8	15	33.3
Total	99	21	13	133	74.4

Summary Statistics: Correct: 90 = 67.7%; $\underline{C}$ = .365; γ = .598; χ^2 = 17.729; d.f. = 2; $\underline{P}$ = .001 (Chi square computed from 3 x 2 table.)

from the data as shown because several of the theoretical frequencies were too small; hence, a 3 x 2 table was made by combining the "Doubtful" and "Poor" columns. The result was 17.729 and $\underline{C}$ was .365. The γ coefficient could be computed directly from the table and was .598. All of these figures are somewhat lower than their counterparts for family relations, but they are not too low. Again, the percentages in the last column of the table confirm the suggestion that motivation can be judged validly from the test; in fact, the 83.3 per cent in the top row came as a surprise to the writer, who has always been hesitant about inferring good motivation from a test like this, which seems in the circumstances of the applicants to invite their putting down what they may know one wants to see. The identification of those with poor motivation is fairly good: there are 13 such, 8 of whom (61.5 per cent) were caught. The designation "Doubt-ful" offers some embarrassment because it was wrong two-thirds of the time; but in practice this is no great diffi-culty since one would merely exercise greater caution with these subjects and be ready to change to a more favorable judgment if the evidence so indicates.

Table 6.4 shows the results when perseverance is taken as the criterion; they are a distinct disappointment. If

Table 6.4

Sentence Completion Test: Motivation and Perseverance

Motivation	*Persevered*	*Left*	*Total*	*Per Cent Persevered*
Good	33	40	73	45.2
Doubtful	14	24	38	36.8
Poor	7	8	15	46.7
Total	54	72	126	42.9

Summary Statistics: $\underline{C}$ = .081; γ = .074; χ^2 = .828; d.f. = 2; $\underline{P}$ = > .50.

the test measures motivation, it is apparently missing some aspects of it which are related to perseverance. It is not that motivation itself has nothing to do with perseverance, a conclusion which is antecedently improbable and contra-dicted by the evidence presented in Chapter 4. A possible explanation is that, in the use of the test, attention has been given to the kind of motivation but not to its intensi-ty, or rather, the firmness with which the candidate holds on to his motives. Hence, an attempt was made to derive a formal scoring method and to include in it a measure of in-tensity.

Formal Scoring for Motivation

From the 1956–1962 groups of novices included in the study of motivation in Chapter 4, those were selected who had been subsequently judged to have either good motivation or poor, doubtful cases being excluded. The test protocols of these men were used for the purpose of deriving a scoring method for both quality and definiteness or determination. Only the the more recent version of the test was used. Various approaches were tried until the following was selected as showing some promise.

119

Scoring for Definiteness or Determination (D):
    (The number of the sentence is given and the stem, then
    the number of points, with norms or typical examples.)
  #2: When the odds are against me--
    2 Fight (try, etc.) even harder (all the harder, etc.),
      like it, like the challenge; try, fight; usually keep
      trying.
    1 Expressions of caution: figure it out, reconsider;
      pray, ask for help.
    0 Give up, yield after trying; do nothing.
  #19: At times I feel--
    2 Any positive expression of confidence, determination,
      etc., provided it is in regard to *vocation*.
    0 Discouraged, depressed, like quitting (not necessarily
      about vocation). Doubts about vocation expressed.
  #24: I worry--
    2 About *acceptance as such* (i.e., indicative of really
      wanting to be accepted).
    0 About vocation, making right choice, perseverance,
      about making grade in studies in the *seminary*.
  #27: If I could only--
    2 Expression of desire of some work done by the order:
      priestly work, teaching, etc. (but not studies, trav-
      el, etc.), ordination, the life in the order. Expres-
      sion of desire of entering the novitiate.
    0 Be certain of vocation.
  #42: I look forward to--
    2 Entering novitiate, teaching, any kind of work of the
      order (but not study, scholarly life, travel, etc.)
    0 Study, vacation, travel, social life (not social
      work), weekend. Expression of doubt or uncertainty
      about vocation.

Scoring for Quality of motivation (Q):
  #12: Most of all I want to--
  #27: If I could only--
  #31: Some day I--
  #42: I look forward to--
  #50: What I want out of life--
    2 *Supernatural and altruistic:* Sacramental or other
      distinctly priestly acts; lead others to God, serve
      God, do will of God. (Not priesthood if mentioned
      alone.)
    1 *Supernatural but selfish* (or, at least, self-center-
      ed):
      Save soul, be a saint, be perfect, be priest (if
      mentioned alone).
      Natural but altruistic: Help others, counsel, etc.

120

(No mention of God, the Faith, etc.)
Natural and selfish (or, at least, self-centered):
Succeed, do something worthwhile, do something with
my life, achieve peace of mind, be happy, be great,
wield influence (unless to help others), be respected.

Note: More than one kind of motivation may be expressed in
one sentence. Each one is scored: v.g., "to save my
soul and help others to save theirs." This response
would be scored 1 for the first part and 2 for the
second.

The sentences were chosen because they frequently elicit
the kind of responses indicated in the scoring norms. Some
others will also prompt similar responses, but these were
ignored in the preliminary work of deriving a scoring system.
Those chosen allow for other completions, often elicit expressions too ambiguous to be scored, or may sometimes be
left blank. This poses a problem. The solution was arrived
at mainly on an empirical basis and was different for the
two variables.

The D score is really a combination of general determination and definiteness in the vocational choice and desire.
General determination, or the lack of it, is usually expressed
in Sentence #2. It was thought that such a general characteristic should be considered pertinent, since the individual
who tends to give up easily may be expected to show this
also in his religious vocation. There was only one score per
response. When a sentence could not be scored, it was not
counted. The final value was the mean of the scorable responses.

For Q it was decided, on the contrary, to allow a score
for each type of motivation expressed in a given completion.
This practice very frequently resulted in two scores for a
sentence and occasionally three. To avoid allowing too much
credit to the more prolific subjects, an averaging method was
tried; but it did not work out as well as the sum of all the
scores, which was then adopted.

After several methods had been tried, both of combining
the D and Q scores and of handling them separately, the sum
of D and Q was selected. In a sense, we are caught in the
embarrassment of adding apples and oranges. This, however,
is what is commonly done in speaking of the adequacy of a
person's motivation: we include both the quality and the
intensity according to some unsystematic manner, which
amounts either to adding the two or balancing them by a
sort of multiplicative function. Actually, the idea of
multiplying the two scores was attractive and was tried--

rather desperately perhaps. There is a further point: the addition involved the *sum* of Q and the *average* of D. This is indeed an odd procedure; but it worked better than any of the others.

Results

The protocols of the two criterion groups were then finally scored according to this method. The results are found in Table 6.5. It will be noted that the "Good" group is subdivided according to perseverance. This was the ex-

Table 6.5

Sentence Completion Test:
Results of Formal Scoring for Motivation: Derivation Group

	Good		Poor (All left)	Per Cent		
Score	Persev.	Left		Total	Good	Perse
9--	2	1		3	100.0	66.
7-8	4	4	1	9	88.9	44.
5-6	4	5	4	13	69.2	30.
3-4	6	10	4	20	80.0	30.
0-2	1	1	9	11	18.2	9.
Total	17	21	18	56	67.9	30.
Mean	4.5	3.8	2.5			

Summary Statistics:
A For Criterion Information: $\underline{C}$ = .249; γ = .483; χ^2 = 3.465; d.f. = 2; $\underline{P}$ = $>$.10 (Chi square from 2 x 3 table.)
B For Perseverance: $\underline{C}$ = .188; γ = .425; χ^2 = 1.987; d.f. = 1; $\underline{P}$ = $>$.10 (Chi square from 2 x 2 table.)

pression of a hope that one might be able to distinguish those whose motivation would hold up from those who would quit when they experienced difficulties. The scores indicated in the firs column need explanation. Since D is an average, the total score often includes one decimal place; but in tabulation the decimal was ignored, so that 2, for example, means 2.0-2.9. This was done with a view to cutting scores which would be easier to recall and apply if they were whole numbers, v.g., below 3. As a result the means, which were computed from grouped scores, are a bit in error: probably too low by about .25 to .50; they are given in the table for illustrative purposes only. The summary statistics are not strictly appropriate for this situation, in which one of the variables is continuous; they are being used primarily for comparison with the other figures used in this chapter.

Two sets of summary figures are given: for the data in the table as such and for the relation of the scores to perseverance. The first may be compared with those in Table 6.3; the second, Table 6.4. In as far as the agreement with the criterion information is concerned, the results are not quite as good as those obtained when the Sentence Completion Test is used impressionistically. But for the prediction of perseverance the situation is very much better. Also, if a cutting score were used and placed at < 3, one fifth (11/56) of the group would be labelled "poor"; the error would be 18 per cent regarding true motivation and 9 per cent as to perseverance. In the middle ranges the score is not very useful for either prediction; at the upper ranges there are too few cases to judge. While these results are not outstanding, the possibility of thus identifying the poor prospects seemed to warrant further investigation.

Cross-Validation

For cross-validation, the 1963-1964 classes were selected, partly because almost all of them had taken the revised form of the test. The scoring procedure was the same, except that the guiding norms were also applied to other sentences than those previously indicated, whenever there was some expression of motivation. The results are presented in Tables 6.6 and 6.7.

Table 6.6

Sentence Completion Test: Results of Formal
    Scoring for Motivation: Cross-Validation Group

Criterion Information

Score	Good	Doubtful	Poor	Total	Per Cent Good
9-13	11			11	100.0
7-8	5			5	100.0
5-6	12		2	14	85.7
3-4	9	4	3	16	56.2
1-2	11	1	1	13	84.6
0		2	2	4	0.0
Total	48	7	8	63	76.2
Mean	5.7	2.3	2.9	5.0	

123

Summary Statistics: $\underline{C}$ = .384; γ = .563; χ^2 = 9.290; d.f. = 1; $\underline{P}$ = .01 (Chi square computed from 2 x 2 table.)

Table 6.7

Sentence Completion Test: Results of Formal Scoring for Motivation: Cross-Validation Group: Perseverance Criterion

Score	Persev.	Left	Total	Per Cent Persevered
9-12	7	1	8	87.5
7-8	1	5	6	16.7
5-6	5	6	11	45.4
3-4	8	7	15	53.3
1-2	8	7	15	53.3
0	3		3	100.0
Total	32	26	58	55.2
Mean	4.6	4.5	4.6	

Summary Statistics: $\underline{C}$ = .056; γ = - .053; χ^2 = .182; d.f. = 1; $\underline{P}$ = .70 (Chi square computed from 2 x 2 table.)

Again, the means are a little inaccurate and the summary statistical indices are not strictly appropriate. Now the prediction of true motivation is a little better than with the preceding group and rather close to what it was with the qualitative interpretation of the test. However, prediction of perseverance falls down completely and the cutting score of < 3 would be completely useless.

Overall, the cross-validation data effectively dispose of the modest promise this formal scoring method had shown with the derivation group. While high scores (5 and above) are closely associated with good motivation, they fail to indicate perseverance unless they reach the level of 9 or more, in which case they pertain to only a small proportion of the whole group. At the lower end, only the zero score indicates doubtful or poor motivation; it involves few subjects; and, ironically, it is associated with perseverance rather than leaving. The percentages in the last column of these tables illustrate better than any of the formal statistical indices how irregular the data are, particularly in regard to perseverance, which is one of the main reasons for devoting so much attention to motivation.

It appears, then, that the formal scoring method does not add much, if anything, to the impressionistic interpretation of the Sentence Completion Test. There seems to be some further discrimination at the upper level, but the criterion information as to true motivation permits only rough distinctions which do not lend themselves well to testing whether this fine discrimination is valid. The scoring method is of no help at the lower end of the motivation continuum, which is really of more concern in screening. And, lastly, prediction of perseverance is made worse rather than improved.

The strategy of multiplying D by Q was appealing as perhaps theoretically more defensible than merely adding them. The zero scores posed a problem. One point was, therefore, added to both D and Q in order to remove the zeroes. The procedure yielded some rather astronomic products, but the results were essentially the same: the high scores were associated with good motivation, there was poor identification in the low scores, and prediction of perseverance was not improved. The details are omitted to save time and space. The general conclusion is that the formal scoring is of no help. In fact, the main and almost sole reason why the results are reported at all is to show that the attempt has been made and perhaps to save someone else a bit of frustration.

Conclusions

In summary, the Sentence Completion Test provides a considerable amount of information that is of help in evaluating a candidate. It reflects family relations fairly accurately. As a means of assessing motivation it does not do as well, but it is of appreciable help. One aspect of motivation that seems to be missed is intensity, i.e., the degree to which the candidate holds firmly to his motives. As a consequence, although motivation is probably the most important factor in perseverance, the test itself does not assess it well enough to tell us who will or will not persevere.

The Sentence Completion Test has to be used with caution, but it can provide leads to many facets, such as general outlook on life, attitudes to other associates besides parents, feelings of inferiority, worries, prepossessions, etc. These have not been subjected to research, partly for lack of time but mainly because what the test elicits varies so much from case to case. And, of course, there would be criterion problems. The leads, and even the fairly clear-cut indications, provided by the test must be checked in the subsequent interview; they are of great value in calling attention to things that might otherwise be overlooked.

Chapter 7

School and College Ability Test

F<small>OR</small> years the A.C.E. Psychological Examination had been
used to gauge scholastic ability. When it was announced that
this would gradually be taken off the market, the School and
College Ability Test (Form 1A) was chosen in its place and
put in use with the class of 1957.

The evidence presented in the publishers' technical manual (Educational Testing Service, 1957) indicates good reliability and validity. The test is of reasonable length.
The administration is rather simple--an important consideration, since it was to be given by men sufficiently acquainted with standardized tests used in high-school guidance but
not trained for the more complex types of test. Early results, however, caused some misgivings because the scores
were generally so high that it did not seem likely that
there was good discrimination of different levels of talent.
And, of course, it is always advisable to check the validity
of a test with a particular group to which it is applied.
Further, there was the question of determining minimum

scores below which the prospect of scholastic success are
too dim to justify admission.

Procedure

Hence, in 1962, a study was made of the classes of 1957-
1958, which by then had completed the novitiate and two years
of full-time classical and literary studies. Those who did
not have the two full years were excluded. Seventy cases
were left, not the highest number desirable but enough for
a reasonably good sample. Only the grades for the two years
were counted. Work taken during the novitiate was excluded
for these reasons: first, the studies in the novitiate are
considered of secondary importance to the spiritual training
which is the primary goal; second, the writer felt the grading
standards were not severe enough; third, some of the courses,
like Latin, served largely as a review of previous work. College grades before entry were ruled out because the SCAT had
been taken after the completion of these courses, except for
a few men who had come from a college which used this test
in its entrance battery. Another reason was the desire to
base the grade averages on a fairly uniform curriculum.

Realization of this last goal was not perfect. There were
two separate houses of study. Furthermore, the students were
divided into an A and a B class according to ability and educational background; these two groups would have been kept
separate had the entire sample been large enough. As a consequence, there are some flaws in the data. The mean grades
are probably overestimates, since the slower students would
tend to be graded higher in competition with their own as
against the faster group. This would also tend to make the
correlations a little lower, and hence underestimates of the
true correlations.

The number of credit-hours attempted varied from 58-91.
Honor points were determined according to the usual method:
i.e., by multiplying the credits for each course by the
honor points given for the grade. The four-point system was
used: 4 points for A, 3 points for B, etc. The honor-point
ratio was the total number of points divided by the number
of credit hours attempted; a grade of F yielded, of course,
no honor points, but the credit-hours were included in the
denominator of the ratio.

Results

The Pearson product-moment correlations (r) which bear
directly on the validity of the SCAT are presented in Table
7.1, together with the means, standard deviations, and
ranges. The correlation of the Total score and grades is

Table 7.1

Correlations of SCAT Scores with Honor-Point Ratio,
    together with Means, Standard Deviations, and Ranges

SCAT:	r	Mean	S.D.	Range
Verbal	.610	309.77*	11.18	281-334
Quantitative	.477	320.37	12.75	274-337
Total	.664	314.41	10.29	288-332
Honor-pt. Ratio		3.01	.55	2.03-3.98

* The SCAT scores given here are scaled scores.

quite good in comparison with the general run of data for
other college ability tests, particularly with a rather
select group. The correlation of the Verbal score with grades
is almost as good as that of the Total. A lower figure was
expected for the Quantitative scale, since the program of
studies consists almost entirely of the languages and other
subjects involving verbal ability. In fact, the r of .477
is surprisingly high under the circumstances.

Since the Total score is obtained by simply adding the
Verbal and Quantitative raw scores and then converting to
scaled scores, it appeared *a priori* possible that better
results could be obtained with some method of weighting the
Verbal and Quantitative scores. The test of such a possibility is the multiple correlation, which provides an
estimate of the best prediction that can be obtained by the
best possible combination of the part scores. The multiple
correlation in this case turned out to be .663. Since the
Total score itself yielded a correlation of .664, it is
clear that nothing would be gained by any procedure of
weighting the part scores differently.

The means indicate that we have a rather talented group.
The "percentile band"[1] equivalents of these means, as determined from the publishers' norms for college freshmen are:
Verbal, 78-91; Quantitative, 74-91; Total, 87-92. The "mid-
percentile ranks" are: Verbal, 85; Quantitative, 85; Total,
89. Achievement is also very good according to the mean
honor-point ratio, which is 3.01. This strikes one as perhaps indicative of lenient grading; but, on the other hand,
the ability level of the group is such that their performance
ought to be quite a bit above average.

Although the mean Total SCAT score is high, the group is
not homogeneously superior. The extent of the spread of scores
is shown in Table 7.2. A little more than two-thirds of the

Table 7.2

Frequency Distribution of SCAT Total Scores

Score	Frequency	Percent	Cumulative Percent
330–334*	4	5.7	5.7
325–329	10	14.3	20.0
320–324	9	12.9	32.9
315–319	17	24.3	57.1
310–314	7	10.0	67.1
305–309	12	17.1	84.3
300–304	4	5.7	90.0
295–299	4	5.7	95.7
290–294	2	2.9	98.6
285–289	1	1.4	100.0

* The highest possible score is 335.

group score 310 or above; a little more than half, 315 or above. In terms of the national norms for Grade 13, Fall Testing, these scores represent percentile bands of 80–87 and 87–92 respectively. Below 305 there is a wide scatter: the lowest person has a converted score of 288, which falls in the percentile band of 20–28.

One would like to determine a point below which promise of success is so slight that the student ought in all charity to be denied admission. But our data are not adequate for this purpose, although they provide some indications. They are not adequate because the primary purpose of this study was to check the validity of the SCAT, and consequently only those subjects were included for whom we had a reasonably satisfactory basis for judging achievement: the full two years of literary studies. Furthermore, all had a passing average (2.00 or better) despite the fact that a few were considered by dean and teachers to be unlikely to succeed in further seminary work. The natural inference seems to be that an average of 2.00 is not enough. But what is enough to serve as a reasonable criterion? It will be necessary to make some assumptions: For their future work, it is desirable that these men obtain at least a Master's degree. To be accepted for graduate studies, they must meet the entrance requirements of some graduate school. Standards vary considerably and are not always clearly indicated in college catalogues, particularly in terms of minimum overall grade-point average. Hence, an absolute norm cannot be set. However, it may be said conservatively that anything less than 2.5 would make it hard to find a school in which acceptance can be gained. Hence, this average will be taken as a working criterion.

Table 7.3 presents data which can be used in choosing a cutting score on the SCAT. This sort of table is called a

Table 7.3

Grade Expectancy for Various SCAT Total Score Intervals*

| | Honor-Point Ratio | | | | |
SCAT Total Score	2.00-2.49	2.50-2.99	3.00-3.49	3.50-3.99	No. of Cases
330-334			25.0	75.0	4
325-329		10.0	10.0	80.0	10
320-324		11.1	55.6	33.3	9
315-319	29.4	29.4	35.3	5.9	17
310-314	14.3	71.4	14.3		7
305-309	16.7	41.7	25.0	16.7	12
300-304	50.0	50.0			4
295-299	50.0	50.0			4
290-294	50.0	50.0			2
285-289	100.0				1
Total	20.0	31.4	24.3	24.3	70

* The figures in the body of the table, columns 2-5, are percentages of those who scored within the given interval on the SCAT. On the assumption that one can generalize to future groups, these percentages may be read as so many chances in 100 of obtaining the grades indicated.

"grade expectancy table" because it can be used as an indication of the likelihood of a certain grade, given a certain aptitude score. The percentages in the body of the table, columns 2-5, may be read as probabilities of obtaining a certain honor-point average; they are thought of as chances in 100. The supposition is, of course, that the data for the group studied will be duplicated at least approximately in subsequent groups. If one reads down the SCAT scale (column 1), it seems that a critical point is reached just below 305, and that there is an uncertain area from that point to 290. The table does not show it, but actually the best cutting point is 302. Sixty-one of the subjects are at or above 302 on the SCAT and nine are below. Eighty-seven percent of the former earned an average of 2.5 or above, while only 33.3 percent of the latter met this criterion. It would seem that anyone scoring below 302 may be regarded as quite doubtful in ability. But, since 33.3 percent would be a fairly appreciable loss of good men if this point were taken as absolute, we should probably consider other evidence, such as the high-school record, before making a decision.[2] There must be a point below which it is of no use to admit a candidate, but we do not have enough data to determine this point with any confidence. Among those who dropped out in the novitiate or first year of studies, nine scored below 302 and one as low as 272; some of these had been doing poorly in their studies. Four of the drop-outs and one of those who persevered fell between 272 and 291. Only one of these did reasonably well; his SCAT score was 288, his honor-point ratio was 2.34, his high-school average was 83.2, and he was described by his master of novices as a hard worker and one of the best of the novices in other respects. Although the evidence is far from conclusive, it would seem that below a score of 292 we need very positive contraindications of ability.

Given the relatively small size of the sample, further research would be desirable. Meanwhile, however, the SCAT has no longer been used routinely; and experimentation with the seminary studies has introduced so much variety in the courses taken by different men that the comparability of their grades has been seriously reduced, if not destroyed. Hence, the conclusions based on this study must remain tentative; they are given for what they are worth.

Conclusions

1 It seems that the SCAT is as satisfactory as any such test.

2 The Total score is the one to use, although the Verbal score is also of help.

3 The group is generally quite superior in ability, but there are several men who are rather mediocre.

4 A Total SCAT score below 302 seems to indicate doubtful scholastic promise. But one should consider previous grades and other standardized-test scores before making a decision to reject an applicant.

5 Below 292 the contrary evidence would have to be very strong before the SCAT score could be set aside. But there are not enough cases to establish an absolute minimum.

Notes

1 The "percentile band" is a kind of score peculiar to this test. It indicates the range in which the subject's true score probably falls, allowance being made for errors of measurement. The "mid-percentile ranks" are the same as the percentile ranks as given in the norms for most tests.

2 It should also be noted that some who are tabulated as below 2.5 are actually very close to that point. However, they are probably offset by those who just barely reached 2.5

References

Cooperative School and College Ability Tests: Technical Report. Princeton, N.J.: Educational Testing Service, 1957.

SCAT-STEP Supplement 1958. Princeton, N.J.: Educational Testing Service, 1958.

SCAT-STEP Supplement 1962. Princeton, N.J.: Educational Testing Service, 1962.

Chapter 8

Study of Values

THE Allport-Vernon-Lindzey Study of Values (1960) was
sed experimentally (Weisgerber, 1966) with the candidates
or one novitiate from 1962-1965. On the face of it, this
est would seem to be very appropriate for the purposes
f screening, since it contains a scale of religious values,
nd the evidence given in the manual shows that clergymen
nd theological students obtain a high mean score on this
cale. McCarthy (1942) had used an earlier edition of it
n one of the first studies of the personality of Cath-
lic seminarians.

Method

The test is based on Spranger's concept of dominant
ife interests and provides measures of the following val-
es: theoretical, economic, aesthetic, social, political,
nd religious. Naturally, one would expect a high score
n the Religious scale in prospective novices and would be
isappointed not to find it; but the experiment required

ignoring the results of the test for the time being, and the writer studiously avoided making any judgment or decision on this basis. A few applicants were not given the test, first, because of a late start in 1962 and, second, because in some cases the available time was needed for a further measure of intelligence, reading, or some other aspect of fitness. There was also an occasional invalid test. Candidates who did not actually enter the novitiate were excluded from further study.

After some preliminary surveys, the data for the 1962-1964 entrants were analyzed in 1965, at which time the first class had completed three years of training; the third class, one year. There were 77 novices in all; 26 had dropped out and 51 still persevered. Fifty-five were high-school graduates; 22 had previously attended college.

The writer's main interest in the test was its relation to motivation; hence the criterion he intended to use was perseverance vs. dropping out. Very soon it became apparent that the test would not serve the purpose of identifying potential drop-outs, yet there was hope it might still have some usefulness in vocational guidance. A control group was then sought in order to determine if there is a difference between those who at least enter the novitiate and those who do not even apply. A group of high-school seniors was given the test by a counselor in a large, urban Catholic high school in the Midwest. Various senior classes were chosen in such a way as to rake the range of ability from the honors class to the slowest. The school is very selective and has a good academic tradition. Although from this standpoint it is not completely representative of Catholic high schools in general, it provided a good control group because those who enter the novitiate are generally in the upper ranges of ability. The restriction of the sample to one school was a matter of availability and time, but this probably introduced no serious error, since the majority of the novices had graduated from a similar school, and the rest, with few exceptions, had attended Catholic high schools in which at least the religious and social atmosphere were comparable The number of subjects was 112, after the exclusion of faulty protocols and two men who later entered the novitiate.

Initially it was assumed that the control group could be compared only with those novices who had entered right after high school. However, when the data were analyzed, it became apparent that the rest could also be included.

Results

Table 8.1 indicates that the Study of Values does not help in identifying potential drop-outs. The scores, as in the remaining tables, are raw scores. None of the differences is statistically significant or, indeed, appre-

Table 8.1

Novices Who Persevered vs. Those Who Dropped Out

| Scale | Persevered | | Dropped Out | | |
	Mean	S.D.	Mean	S.D.	t
Theoretical	38.23	6.85	37.08	8.11	.644
Economic	31.00	6.44	33.72	6.72	1.699
Aesthetic	34.94	7.25	37.92	8.48	1.589
Social	44.41	5.99	42.15	6.89	1.466
Political	39.82	5.20	39.21	5.99	.458
Religious	51.58	5.69	49.92	6.42	1.141
	($\underline{N}$=51)		($\underline{N}$=26)		

Note—None of the differences in means is significant at the 5% level.

ciable. Since profile analysis is often useful even when scores on any single scale are not, an attempt was made at

Table 8.2

High-School vs. College Subgroups in Novice Sample

| Scale | High School | | College | | |
	Mean	S.D.	Mean	S.D.	t
Theoretical	37.61	7.59	38.41	6.57	.428
Economic	32.58	6.52	30.25	6.72	1.387
Aesthetic	35.62	7.63	36.77	8.19	.579
Social	43.24	6.20	44.68	6.76	.889
Political	40.13	5.22	38.34	5.91	1.288
Religious	50.81	5.56	51.55	6.95	.481

Note—None of the differences in means is significant at the 5% level.

this approach. The raw scores were converted to T scores based on means and standard deviations reported in the manual, and the profiles were sorted according to the highest scale. The perseverance rate of those whose Religious scale score is highest proves to be a little better (81.8 per cent) than the rate for the rest of the group (75.0 per cent) but this difference is not significant.

Candidates from high school and those from college are compared in Table 8.2; again, there is no significant difference. Hence, the data from these two groups can be combined, and we have some assurance that the control group, although it includes no college students, is reasonably adequate for our purpose.

Table 8.3 gives the means of the novices--all who entered --and the control group. Five of the differences in means

Table 8.3

Novices vs. Control Group

	Novices		Controls		
Scale	*Mean*	*S.D.*	*Mean*	*S.D.*	*P*
Theoretical	37.84	7.32	41.57	6.31	.001
Economic	31.92	6.66	40.05	7.50	.001
Aesthetic	35.95	7.81	34.31	6.86	.14
Social	43.65	6.40	39.67	6.87	.001
Political	39.62	5.48	43.43	6.39	.001
Religious	51.02	6.00	41.00	7.33	.001

are significant at well beyond the .001 level. The novices are significantly higher on the Religious and Social scales; higher (but not significantly) on the Aesthetic; significantly lower on the Economic, Theoretical, and Political. Most important is the fact that the novices are ten points higher than the controls on the Religious scale; perhaps also important is the difference in the other direction on the Economic. To clarify these differences, frequency distributions were made for these scales; they are shown in Table 8.4. The Religious scale separates the two groups rather well: 63.6 per cent of the novices scored 50 or higher as against only 10.7 per cent of the controls; 10.4 per cent of the novices were below 45, and 67.9 per cent of the controls. The novices tend to concentrate at the upper end of the scale, 45-65; and this restriction of the range of their scores is probably the reason why one cannot discriminate

136

potential drop-outs. On the Economic scale, while the controls are consistently higher, the overlap of the distributions is too great for any practical use.

Table 8.4

Distribution of Scores of Novices and Controls
    on Religious and Economic Values Scales

| | Religious Values | | Economic Values | |
Score	Novices	Controls	Novices	Controls
60–65	3.9%			
55–59	24.7	1.8%		2.7%
50–54	35.1	8.9		7.1
45–49	26.0	21.4	1.3%	17.9
40–44	6.5	25.9	15.6	27.7
35–39	2.6	27.7	20.8	25.9
30–34		9.8	26.0	8.9
25–29	1.3	3.6	22.1	8.0
20–24			9.1	.9
15–19			5.2	.9
5–14		.9		

The Study of Values does not provide a basis for predicting which novices are likely to drop out, and hence is probably of little use for screening purposes. On the other hand, this finding is not inconsistent with the data which the test's authors give in support of the validity of the Religious value scale, since men who aspire to a priestly vocation ought to have high religious values and apparently do for the most part. Although a longer follow-up period may be theoretically desirable, the trend of the data and the concentration of novices in the higher score ranges of this scale make it highly improbable that the present results would be reversed. Possibly those with comparatively low scores may still drop out, as did one man with a score of 27; but there are so few that a very large total number of cases would be required for an adequate statistical test. Furthermore, economy of time would militate against routine testing with such a minute return for one's efforts.

However, the clear difference between novices and controls in means and in distribution of scores on the Religious value scale suggests that the test may be of help at an earlier stage of vocational planning. Those who score high are clearly similar in their religious values to the group who actually entered the novitiate; they should perhaps consider a religious vocation. Twelve of the controls, for example, received a score of 50-59, which placed them at or above the mean of the novices; the counselor might well have informed these men of the fact and asked them if they had considered the priesthood or the religious life. Any action more definite than this would, of course, run counter to good principles of counseling and of religious guidance.

On the basis of the differences shown in Table 8.3, and assuming the validity of the test, we may attempt a description of the values of the typical novice. His dominant values are religious. The social are next, i.e., he has an altruistic love of people, is kind, sympathetic, and unselfish. He is rather uninterested in money, economics, business, in the purely utilitarian things of life. He does not want to dominate men or achieve personal power. He is less concerned with theoretical and intellectual matters than perhaps he should be. He is sensitive to beauty and art about as much as his peers.

In this discussion it should be noted that the Study of Values is a so-called *ipsative* scale; i.e., the measurements depend first and primarily on a comparison of different trends within the individual rather than an immediate comparison with a group. The answers to the test items call for a preference of one thing over another. For example, the second item reads: "Taking the Bible as a whole, one should regard it from the point of view of its beautiful mythology and literary style rather than as a spiritual revelation. (a) Yes; (b) No." If the answer is "Yes," the Aesthetic score goes up; the Religious score, down; and conversely if the answer is "No." It is possible for two men to make the same choice yet differ in the intensity of their allegiance to the value in question. As a consequence, the test tells us which of the six value systems comes out ahead for the individual, but does not assure us that this value is adhered to tenaciously. Herein lies perhaps another reason why the Religious scale does not identify drop-outs. It also means that the novices and controls can be compared in regard to what values dominate and to what extent they dominate, but not as to intensity of adherence to these values--at least not directly.

It is risky to generalize from the present results to other groups. Neither the novice nor the control group is a random sample; and one is derived from a specific religious order, the other, from a specific high school in one part of the country. The writer has no reason for regarding the present group as anything but typical of the novices he has been screening for some dozen years. However, he would be hesitant to assert that they are also typical of the novices of even the same religious order in other parts of the country.

Similarly, the high-school students may not be representative of those attending Catholic high schools throughout the country. At any rate, it is almost axiomatic in the use of tests for selection and guidance, to obtain empirical evidence of their predictive validity for each new group or situation to which they are applied.

Conclusions

With these reservations in mind, we may conclude:
1 The Allport-Vernon-Lindzey Study of Values is not useful for identifying potential drop-outs among those who enter a religious order.

2 It may be helpful, nevertheless, in vocational guidance and counseling: high scores on the Religious value scale may call attention to the possibility of a vocation to the priesthood or religious life.

3 Novices, in comparison with a control group, stand out as notably high in Religious values and to a lesser extent in Social; they are quite low in Economic.

As a result of this investigation, the use of the test was discontinued after the 1965 class. Since the completion of the data analysis in late 1965, the test profiles of those who have since left the order have been examined. There was no indication of any change in the trend of the results; hence no attempt was made to increase the size of the sample by including the last class.

References

Allport, Gordon W., Vernon, Philip E., and Lindzey, Gardner. *Manual: Study of Values: A Scale for Measuring the Dominant Interests in Personality*. Third edition. Boston: Houghton Mifflin, 1960.
McCarthy, Thomas J. Personality traits of seminarians. *Stud. Psychol. Psychiat., Cath. U.*, 1942, 5, No. 4.
Weisgerber, Charles A., S.J. The Study of Values in screening for a religious order. *J. Relig. & Hlth*, 1966, 5, 233-38.

Chapter 9

Predictors

I⊤ has been shown in previous chapters that several factors in the case history or the tests are associated with a poor rate of perseverance or with a good. This finding suggests the use of such factors to aid prediction. While one of these, motivation, seems to override all the others and might conceivably be used by itself, it appeared advisable to develop a system which would take all of them into account, both negative and positive. Hence attempts were made to combine these various indicators.

Method

The data from the 1959-1962 classes were used. At the time, 57.8 per cent had persevered; hence, the base rate, in terms of probability independently of any predictors, was taken as .58 for perseverance and .42 for leaving. Those factors were selected for which the perseverance rate was notably better than .58 or the drop-out rate notably worse than .42. The base rate was subtracted from the obtained proportion of persevering (for the positive factor) or leaving (for the negative). The result was divided by the base rate to yield a percentage of improvement. Weights were then assigned according to the following scheme: 1 for ten to nineteen per cent; 2 for twenty to twenty-nine, etc. By way of example, let us take the figures for a K raw score of 9 or less. Of those who displayed this feature in the MMPI profile, 60 per cent left; probability of leaving was taken, therefore, as .60; the base rate was .42; improvement (in prediction) over the base rate was .18; divided by .42, this was 43 per cent; a weight of 4 was assigned. The weights are minus for the poor, plus for the good indicators. Only those factors were retained for which the number of cases was at least 20. With those drawn from the MMPI, the cross-validation procedure had been used, as described in Chapter 3; they were eliminated if they did not survive cross-validation.

A list of good and poor indicators was drawn up, as shown in Table 9.1. Unfortunately, the number of good indi-

Table 9.1

Poor and Good Indicators of Perseverance

	Probability of Leaving	Weight
Poor Indicators:		(minus)
Motivation poor or questionable*	.92	11
Family relations poor	.66	5
Family relations fair	.52	2
Scrupulous (actively)	.64	5
Late application (July or August)	.68	6
K Raw Score: $\leq$ 9	.60	4
$\leq$ 10	.53	2
$\leq$ 11	.56	2**
MMPI high point code: 4	.64	5
4 in first two (and ties for 2nd)	.51	2
K $\leq$ 13 & SD $\leq$ 24 (raw scores)	.62	4
Good Indicators:		(plus)
MMPI high point code: 6	.35	1
2	.34	1
3	.33	1
MMPI low point code: 8	.25	2
2	.32	1

* & **, page 142.

* Definitions of terms for the first five factors are
given in Chapter 4.
   ** Adjusted because of the reversal of the probability
figures (.53 and .56).

cators is slight in comparison with the poor; but this seems
only to reflect the observed fact that it is harder to identify the really good prospects than those who are risky.
The table also demonstrates the preponderance of case-history
information.

Various methods of applying the predictors were tried:
taking only the highest negative or positive probability,
highest negative weight, average of the probabilities, the
ratio of negative to positive weights, and, finally, the
algebraic sum of the weights. The last method worked best
and was adopted.

The system was first tried with the records of those
in the class of 1963 whom the writer had interviewed himself. It showed promise. Then the classes of 1962, 1964,
and 1965 were added, with the same restriction. The method
is now being applied tentatively with all cases, although
it is likely to be ineffective with those not seen by the
writer, since information regarding motivation, family, and
scrupulosity is less than adequate in most of these cases.

The scoring procedure, then, is to examine the records
for the information required, to note down the plus and
minus weights, and to take their algebraic sum. In each
group a few will have no plusses or minuses; they are given
a zero score. The case-history factors are often somewhat
hard to judge, particularly family relations and motivation.
In the latter case there are two major sources of doubt:
first, the quality of motivation, i.e., whether it is primarily supernatural or natural, altruistic or selfish; second, its intensity. One can get some information regarding
the first question from the Sentence Completion Test, the
autobiography, and the interview, although often enough
this is by no means easy. As to intensity, the present techniques leave one almost completely in the dark. (Cf. the unsuccessful attempt to meet this problem in Chapter 6.) In
addition, there are difficulties inherent in a more or less
mechanical method. Cut-off points have to be specified; how
much error is introduced when one counts, let us say, any
K score at or below 11 and ignores a score of 12?

Results

There is, as yet, no adequate body of data to test the
method. The 1963 group, as indicated above, was used for

the pilot study. Going back to 1962 involved dipping into the cases from which the probability figures were obtained. The 1964 and 1965 classes are probably too recent. At the risk of finding what one hoped to find, data for the 1962-1963 classes were analyzed (see Table 9.2). Those for 1964-1965 are presented (Table 9.3) as a possible check on these results. The method was also applied to the candidates for the brothers in the same order from 1962-1965 (Table 9.4).

Table 9.2

Results of Predictor System, 1962-1963

Score	Persevered	Left	Total
+2 to -1	10	7	17
-2 to -5	9	5	14
-6 to -9	4	6	10
-10 to -13	1	8	9
-14 to -24		2	2
Total	24	28	52
Mean	-2.42	-6.64	-4.69
S.D.	3.45	5.50	5.12

Note--Point biserial correlation, corrected for coarse grouping: .498; $\underline{P}$ .001.

Table 9.3

Results of Predictor System, 1964-1965

Score	Persevered	Left	Total
+2 to -1	14	10	24
-2 to -5	9	4	13
-6 to -9	4	1	5
-10 to -13	1	5	6
-14 to -17	2	1	3
Total	30	21	51
Mean	-2.93	-4.48	-3.57
S.D.	4.49	5.52	5.00

Note--Point biserial correlation, corrected for coarse grouping: .190; $\underline{P}$: $>$.10.

Table 9.4

Results of Predictor System with Brothers, 1962-1965

Score	Persevered	Left	Total
+2 to -1	3	2	5
-2 to -5	4	3	7
-6 to -9	1	2	3
-10 to -13		7	7
-14 to -17	1	4	5
-18 to -31		3	3
Total	9	21	30
Mean	-4.22	-11.24	-9.13
S.D.	4.64	8.16	7.97

Note--Point biserial correlation, corrected for coarse grouping: .489; $\underline{P}$: .01.

The numbers of cases are small for the purpose: 52, 51, and 30 respectively.

With the first group the results are promising, the point biserial correlation corrected for coarse grouping is .498. This statistic drops to a mere .190 with the 1964-1965 men and appears to negate the promise indicated by the previous figure. However, for the brothers it is again rather good, .489. The distribution of scores in Tables 9.2 and 9.4 suggests that a cut-off point of about -10 would be effective, but this is not true of the data in Table 9.3.

It is probably too early to evaluate this method of prediction with any confidence. It will be necessary to wait two years or more for further drop-outs: had the 1963 results, for example, been tabulated one year earlier they would have been less favorable and would have lowered the .498 correlation quite a bit. In this regard the brothers are a more convenient group to work with. Those who leave tend to make up their minds earlier, and it is not necessary to wait so long before a follow-up study. At any rate the indications are at present ambiguous: the method may or may not work, and time will have to decide the issue.

Chapter 10

Brothers

Hᴇʀᴇᴛᴏꜰᴏʀᴇ, we have been considering only candidates
destined for the priesthood, except for the data in Table
9.4. Initially the brothers were not given the psychological
tests. The reasons for this are not on record. According to
Canon Law, they must first go through a postulancy of six
months before admission to the novitiate; very likely this
was thought to provide sufficient chance to judge their
suitability. In late 1956 a number of changes were made in
the admission procedure, and at this time it was decided to
include the brothers in the screening program. This was essentially the same as for the other candidates, except for
the use of the Army General Classification Test (AGCT),
First Civilian Edition (1948). This was chosen for several
reasons: Since it was used successfully with some 12,000,000
army inductees in World War II, it provides a good basis of
comparison with the general population. Secondly, it is of
reasonable length and comparatively foolproof in administration. Third, it entails three types of content: vocabulary,
arithmetic, and reasoning about spatial relations, rather

than just one kind of material. Fourth, the applicants for the brotherhood are of varying ages, educational background, and work experience; some of them have been out of school for a number of years. Hence the usual type of scholastic aptitude test would be inappropriate in many cases, whereas the AGCT was standardized with just such a disparate group. Fifth, norms are available for college entrants and can be used when the situation calls for an estimate of college ability. And last, separate scores can be obtained for the three parts of the test (Barnette, 1955), which are helpful both in the clinical interpretation of the results and in later use for guidance purposes.

Testing for Special Aptitudes

At about the same time plans were made for a battery of tests to determine aptitude for specific lines of work the brothers might do. These were mostly: food service, mechanical and maintenance, infirmarian work, clerical-secretarial and bookkeeping, farming-gardening and grounds-keeping, or domestic. The best choice for the purpose would undoubtedly have been the General Aptitude Test Battery of the U.S. Employment Service; in fact, a number of the brothers had been given these through the courtesy of the local branch of this service. But the test is not for sale. After a survey of the literature the Flanagan Aptitude Classification Tests (FACT) were adopted. These covered a majority of the jobs brothers would be doing. Aside from being difficult to administer, they are open to the objection that the oldest group for whom norms are given are high-school seniors; but this is true also of most published batteries on the market. Validity, of course, was a problem, since the test was new at the time. The Differential Aptitude Tests were originally ruled out because they were not so closely related to most of the manual jobs assigned to the brothers. However, in recent years it has been added and some of the FACT subtests have been dropped. The increasing number of brothers who are likely to go into work requiring some college education was the main consideration; the score combination entitled "Verbal Reasoning plus Numerical Reasoning" is a good indicator of college aptitude. (Incidentally, this test also does not have norms beyond high school.) The Kuder Preference Record, Vocational, Form C was the principal interest measure. A background information form has also been employed (cf. Appendix E).

These were the heart of the program. The AGCT, as previously indicated, was also of some help. The MMPI results were considered in making recommendations, particularly if more stressful jobs were being considered, such as that of infirmarian. Initially, the Shipley-Institute of Living Scale was used as a further check on general ability; the Thurstone Interest Schedule, as a check on the Kuder. Occasionally, other tests were added, such as the Strong Vocational Interest Blank, the Minnesota Clerical Test, one of the Otis series, a reading test, and so forth. The Shipley and Thurstone tests have been dropped. The Minnesota Vocational Interest Inventory (Clark and Campbell, 1965) has recently been added, and consideration is now being given to a new form of the Kuder (DD) which includes scores for many interests in the academic sphere.

In the use of these tests, one runs into the usual problems which plague the guidance counselor: disparity between interests as measured and as the individual sees them, lack of correspondence between interest and aptitude, low apparent aptitude vs. good high-school achievement in related subjects, choice between occupational and avocational plans, and so forth. But the basic problem has been the validity of the tests. In general, the test batteries on the market have been difficult to validate in terms of actual performance later and have not proven as successful as was hoped in differentiating the various hypothetical special aptitudes. This last weakness is particularly acute with those who appear good at almost everything and those who are consistently poor. But the main difficulty has been the lack of sufficient numbers of cases for a check of validity. Hence, the program is merely described here for the information of any who may be considering this sort of testing.

Results of Screening

To return to the admission screening, the brothers were not followed up in the same way as the candidates for the priesthood until rather recently. This was due simply to lack of time, so much of it being committed to the other research and testing. Hence, it will be necessary to content ourselves for the present with the criterion of perseverance. There were 83 who had been examined and admitted from 1956 to 1963. This number includes two who had first entered with the priesthood in mind. The only exclusion was the case of a man with a foreign-language background.

The results are given in Table 10.1. The judgment therein referred to was made after the interview in 42 cases; on the basis of the tests alone in 41. The reason for combining the data in this way was simply to have a reasonably sufficient total. A separate tabulation showed that the two groups do not differ much. The data are similar

147

Table 10.1

Success of Predictions against Criterion of Perseverance

Judgment	Persev.	Left	Total	Per Cent Persev
Satisfactory	22	26	48	45.8
Doubtful	8	24	32	25.0
Unsatisfactory	1	2	3	33.3
Total	31	52	83	37.4

Summary Statistics: $\underline{C}$ = .205; γ = .390; χ^2 = 3.501; $\underline{P}$ = .10.

to those obtained with the candidates for the priesthood, except that it is somewhat clearer in Table 10.1 that those judged doubtful or unsatisfactory generally fail to measure up. Also, the identification of those who will leave is better; just half of them as against twenty-nine per cent at best for the other candidates (cf. Chapter 2, Table 2.12, Group A).

Many of the brothers are older and have a varied background. Some have been attracted to this vocation because of dissatisfaction with their previous way of living and wish to find a goal in life which will really have meaning to them. In most instances this is perfectly normal; occasionally there is question of definite maladjustment to the demands of secular life. Hence, a greater need for caution. With the younger men there are some problems too, particularly when achievement in school has been irregular and below their apparent ability. It seemed worthwhile, therefore, to determine the number of "bad misses" as against "hits," as was done in Chapter 2. The same distinction between mental illness and other undesirable conditions was used and the same criteria (cf. pp. 45-48), with the following exceptions: One man was mentally ill before the application, rather than having become ill afterwards; but it was obvious in the interview that he was still quite seriously disturbed. A second was rejected on psychiatric advice. Three had attempted to hold back important information. In several cases there was difficulty deciding whether mental illness as such was involved; for example, one of those who attempted deception had been in a mental hospital, but he was classified under "other conditions" because lying about it was the immediate reason for rejection. In doubt, the milder classification was used.

The results, indicated in Table 10.2, are much like those in Table 2.19, Chapter 2. However, they show a little better success: on the average two clearly undesirable cases are

Table 10.2

Undesirable Candidates Caught and Missed by the Screening

Years	Mental Illness		Other Conditions		Both Combined		Total Examined
	Caught	*Missed*	*Caught*	*Missed*	*Caught*	*Missed*	
1956-1959	2		4	1	6	1	51
1960-1963	1	2	10	2	11	4	68
Total	3	2	14	3	17	5	119
Per Year	.4	.2	1.8	.4	2.1	.6	

caught annually and one is missed every other year. The record for detecting mental illness does not appear quite this good, but the conservative policy mentioned above is partly responsible for the difference; two cases could without any stretching have been counted as "hits" under the heading of "mental illness." With the brother candidates we run into more cases of clearcut unfitness than with the others, and accordingly we have a wider range on the scale of fitness-unfitness. As in similar cases of personnel selection, this makes it possible to show a better record of success.

The table, as it is organized, may give the impression that the screening is getting less rather than more effective in regard to detecting mental illness. While this is not impossible--actually all but one of the clear "misses" have been in the last three years--it is most likely a matter of normal fluctuation. Ten of the 17 "hits" are also concentrated in a period of three years, 1960-1962. Lastly, it must be noted that there is probably considerable error in the data due to inadequate information on the subsequent careers of many of the men. This would not much affect the balance of success in the mental illness category because the writer was generally consulted or informed if serious emotional trouble arose. But it could mean that some of his less serious mistakes did not come to his attention.

Army General Classification Test

Data in regard to the Army General Classification Test are presented in Table 10.3. The results have been organized with two things in mind: the general level of intelli-

Table 10.3

Distribution of AGCT Scores of Brothers Admitted, 1957-1964

Score	Number of Cases P*	L	Tot.	Cumulative Percentage P	L	Tot.
140---		4	4		100.0	100.0
135-139	3	4	7	100.0	92.7	95.2
130-134	3	4	7	89.7	85.5	86.9
125-129	4	3	7	79.3	78.2	78.6
120-124	5	11	16	65.5	72.7	70.2
115-119	4	9	13	48.3	52.7	51.2
110-114	1	5	6	34.5	36.4	35.7
105-109	4	6	10	31.0	27.3	28.6
100-104	2		2	17.2	16.4	16.7
95-99	1		1	10.3	16.4	14.3
90-94	1	2	3	6.9	16.4	13.1
85-89		1	1	3.4	12.7	9.5
80-84	1	1	2	3.4	10.9	8.3
---79		5	5		9.1	6.0
Total	29	55	84			
Mean	117.38	114.59	115.55			
S.D.	13.21	20.25	18.18			

* P = persevered; L = left.

gence of these men and the determination of a likely minimum score for future applicants. In this test, the raw score
is converted to a standard score with a mean of 100 and a
standard deviation of 20. According to the usual procedures
in constructing intelligence tests, a standard score of 100
ought to correspond to an IQ of 100. However, the standard
deviation of most tests that yield an IQ is 15 or 16, rather than 20. Hence, the AGCT scores are not closely comparable to IQs when they are much above or below 100. Percentiles are also given for the general population and for college entrants.

It is clear that the brothers as a group are considerably above average: their general mean is 115.55, which
would be at about the 75th percentile for men in general
and the 32nd for college. Only 14 per cent of the group
scored below 100, and three-fourths of these left the order.
About 70 per cent had a score of 110 or above. This has a
bearing on relations within the group, since the less able
would tend to have difficulty fitting in. It would also
affect their training, whether academic or spiritual,
since it is not easy to reach simultaneously the very slow

and the very bright. Incidentally, the mean of those who persevered is not quite three points higher than the mean of those who left; but the difference is not significant either statistically or practically.

The interest in a minimum score below which rejection of applicants would be recommended was prompted by the opinion of some vocation promoters that the brother candidate should be at least of average intelligence. While one cannot logically argue from what has been to what should be, it seems that this opinion is in accord with the data. A minimum score should never be applied mechanically. However, 100 may be used as a cut-off, with careful scrutiny of other evidence and balancing strengths in any who fall below this point. Below 90 the chances of success are rather slight.

References

Barnette, W. Leslie, Jr. Diagnostic features of the AGCT. *J. Soc. Psychol.*, 1955, 42, 241-47.

Berger, Raymond M., and Lytle, Ruth. *Technical Report for the First Civilian Edition of the AGCT (Army General Classification Test)*. Chicago: Science Research Associates, 1960.

Clark, Kenneth E., and Campbell, David P. *Minnesota Vocational Interest Inventory, Manual*. New York: Psychological Corp., 1965.

Examiner Manual for the Army General Classification Test, First Civilian Edition. Revised, November 1948. Chicago: Science Research Associates, 1948.

Chapter 11

General Conclusions

After the consideration of a large mass of detailed
and sometimes conflicting data, it is necessary to draw
together the general conclusions that emerge. The summary
will have to be selective. In order to make it easy to refer back to the sections on which the conclusions are based,
they will be presented in the same order as the preceding
chapters.

Overall Effectiveness (Chapter 2)

In the report to the superior on the results of the
personality assessment of each candidate, the psychologist
made a summary judgment of the fitness of the man for the
religious life from the standpoint of mental health and
personality. This was expressed by the terms: "satisfactory," "doubtful," or "unsatisfactory"--or their equivalents.
It was the correctness of these judgments which was investigated first. Information regarding the subsequent careers
of the religious was classified according to the following
criteria: mental health, overall adjustment, perseverance,

and reaching ordination. These four criteria yielded about the same results; there were exceptions, but they could easily be due to chance.

1 The percentage of correct judgments made by the psychologist varies somewhat with the criterion and the group of candidates studied: 60-70 for the earlier classes and 50-65 for the later. Improvement over the base rate varies from -2 to +8 per cent. (The base rate is the actual percentage satisfactory, doubtful, or unsatisfactory in the whole group, regardless of the psychologist's judgments. And similarly for the criteria of perseverance and ordination. It provides an estimate, although somewhat biased against favorable results, of what the percentages would be without the screening.)

2 The situation is a little different when one considers separately the actual content of the psychologist's verdict. With those he judged satisfactory he was right in 60-75 per cent of the cases in the earlier classes and 50-70 in the later. Improvement over the base rate was 3-4 per cent. With those he declared doubtful or unsatisfactory the percentage correct was 40-70 and 50-70 for an improvement of 10-25. Hence, the unfavorable predictions are more successful than the favorable.

3 However, of those who did turn out to be less than satisfactory, only 20-30 per cent were actually identified in advance. This demonstrates a notable weakness in the screening procedures.

4 Results with the program are better than without it, but how much better they are depends on the precise criterion used, one's understanding of the goal of the process, and from what aspect the data are viewed. The writer takes the position that the main object is to identify the unsuited, and in this regard the improvement achieved is 10-25 or 20-30 per cent according to the figures just given in #2 and #3. This is disappointing indeed.

5 A somewhat more favorable indication of accuracy was found with a group of fifty cases in which the master of novices stated in his report that he thought the psychologist was right or wrong. The percentage correct was 64. This is no better than the previous figures; but there were instances in which the psychologist was mostly correct, and the addition of these raises the percentage to 80. This is rather good, although it is perhaps a little too high because of the influence of suggestion.

6 Data comparing results of the tests (and allied written sources of information) with those after a psychological interview failed to show any advantage in general predictive validity for the latter. But the interview does correct the test results in an appreciable number of cases, although it misses

153

a larger proportion of the poor risks than one should like. There are other considerations, not demonstrable by hard facts, which are in favor of the interview.

7 A final consideration was the prior identification of serious risks, particularly those who demonstrate themselves clearly unfit in regard to mental health, but also those who show a serious failure in some other aspect of adjustment. In an earlier study published in 1962, it was shown that one or two such people were caught per year but that on the average a little more than two were missed. For a later group, the results were similar: about one caught per year and two missed, when mental health as such is considered. However, for other conditions which also entail a serious failure in adjustment, five are caught annually and eight are missed. (It should be noted that those described as caught were not necessarily excluded from the novitiate; but the psychologist had marked them as unsatisfactory or doubtful.)

8 The final, general conclusion seems to be that the psychological screening is better than nothing at all. However, it cannot be shown to be strikingly better. It is missing far too many poor risks. In view of the rather modest results, it is a matter of a value judgment whether to continue or drop the procedure--aside, of course, from efforts to improve it.

The MMPI (Chapter 3)

The MMPI was investigated rather thoroughly over the course of the years. Quite a bit of detailed information has been obtained, much of which will have to be passed over in this summary.

1 If normalized T scores are used in place of the linear type, the results they yield are essentially the same. They reduce, it is true, the number of deviant profiles one obtains and the extent of the deviation, but they decrease predictive value.

2 It is apparent from results of the 1962 study that candidates who persevere do not differ appreciably from those who leave, in regard to their mean scores on the various MMPI scales. The profile of the means is similar to that obtained with college students, but generally a little higher. Mf, Pd, and Sc are the highest scales and show the greatest increase over college samples.

3 If profile analysis is applied, i.e., considering not means but which scale is highest for the individual, Mf, Pd, Sc, and Ma are the most frequent--and in that order.

Profiles with other scales as the highest point are not very common. On the basis of the one highest scale alone, it seems impossible to predict the criteria of mental health, overall adjustment, or perseverance. (But see the conclusions from the later group.)

4 If we also consider the second-highest scale and a few other combinations, we find some promise of help. Although the results vary slightly with the different criteria, the following combinations appear to suggest a poor chance of perseverance or adjustment to the religious life: as the two highest, Mf and Ma, or Pd and Ma; Pd, Mf, and Ma as the three highest regardless of their order; Pd highest and at a $\underline{T}$ score of 70 or above; and perhaps also Pd and Sc as the two highest.

5 Data for later classes (1956-1962) are taken from a further revision of the MMPI by Bier and involve corrections in the scoring keys and special norms prepared by the writer. Hence, they cannot be compared exactly with the earlier data. However, with this group also, a high point on Pd again seems unfavorable, although there is some inconsistency in the data. The unfavorable patterns are: Pd at 70 or above, D first and Si second-highest, Pa highest and Hy second to it, Pd and Ma the two highest (in either order), and generally Pd as highest or second highest. The favorable profiles are: D or Hy or Pa highest, Hy highest and Pa second, Pa highest and D lowest, D highest and Ma lowest. (In all these, the criterion was perseverance.)

6 It was noted earlier (#3, #4) that the candidates tended to be high on Mf, Pd, Sc, and Ma. They were also high on K. While these scales, except for Ma, were not so prominent among the later group (1956-1962) because of the change in norms, some attention was given to Pd, K, and Ma. It was found that Pd tends to be associated with poorer observance of religious discipline and rules, as would be expected on the basis of its intended meaning. The K scale reflects good adjustment. Some of the data suggest a curvilinear relation, with moderate scores favorable and both low and high scores unfavorable. But the results are not consistent, except that, if the raw score is at least below 10, poor adjustment and lack of perseverance are indicated. The relation of Ma to perseverance is similar: a suggestion of a curvilinear relation in some data, a linear in other data, but with the lower scores (below a $\underline{T}$ of 40) indicative of a *good* chance of perseverance.

7 Among the experimental scales, SD, A, R, Se, and Wa were investigated, either alone or in some combinations. Low SD (Social Desirability) with low K makes for poor adjustment and lack of perseverance, but by itself it does

not help prediction and it adds very little to what is obtained with K alone. A (Anxiety) is inversely related to perseverance, as one might have expected. R (Repression) is not correlated with this criterion; it may possibly have some effect in combination with A, but the data are too sparse. The Se (Seminary) Scale, which gave good results for its author, is of no value with our groups. Wa (Work Attitude) shows some relation to motivation and perseverance, but it does not seem to be good enough for our purposes.

Motivational, Background, and Other Factors (Chapter 4)

The following were investigated: motivation, family relations, late application, and age. Motivation was considered poor if it was not sufficiently supernatural and altruistic, or not genuine. Poor family relations meant a serious family disturbance, whether of objective record like divorce or more a matter of subjective attitudes like serious resentment against a parent. A candidate was rated as scrupulous if he showed the usual symptoms at the time he was examined or had shown them previously for a notable period of time. Late application was understood as reaching the point of taking the psychological tests in July, August, or September. Age was computed as of the date of entry. The conclusions:

1 Poor or questionable motivation is the most salient feature in the entire record, showing a dropout rate of 92 per cent. But good motivation, at least as judged by the psychological examiner, is no guarantee of perseverance, since about half of those initially well motivated failed to persevere.

2 Family relations are next in importance: the dropout rate was two-thirds for those whose family relations were poor in some way, and this despite the variety of disturbances included under the rubric.

3 The dropout rate for the scrupulous was also about two-thirds; and similarly for late applicants.

4 Age did not show any relation to perseverance.

Time Aspects (Chapter 5)

An attempt was made to determine if those likely to leave the novitiate early (within the first three months) could be detected in advance. A second question concerned the time span over which one might hope the predictions to hold good: i.e., whether it were really possible to exclude those who might have serious psychological problems in the distant future. For this latter question perseverance had to be used

as the criterion, despite the criticism that its connection
with adjustment is indirect and not universal.

1 The factors identified with early leaving are the
same as those associated with leaving at any time. None
stands out, with the possible exception of poor motivation.

2 Since poor or doubtful motivation indicates with a
high degree of probability those who will leave eventually,
if not early, it appears to be a sufficient reason for postponement of admission.

3 Late application or a $\underline{T}$ score of at least 70 on the
Pd scale of the MMPI should prompt one to caution but not
rejection or deferral of the candidate.

4 As far as short-term or long-term prediction is concerned, the record is best for the immediate future, i.e.,
the first year, although even that is not very good. Perhaps
this span can be extended to the fourth year. Beyond this
point in time the evidence is inconclusive: there is an
intermediate period in which leaving the order seems to have
nothing to do with the psychologist's original rating, but
there is also a suggestion that the men who leave toward
the end of the years of training are more often those who
had been rated unfavorably. However, more data are needed
before one can decide for or against the possibility of
long-term prediction.

Sentence Completion Test (Chapter 6)

It is difficult to make an adequate study of the Sentence Completion Test. No data on its reliability are presented. Data have been offered as to its validity in assessing motivation and family relations. Also a formal method
of scoring for motivation was attempted.

1 The test reflects family relations fairly accurately, being correct in 62 per cent of the cases.

2 As a means of assessing motivation it does not do
as well, but is of appreciable help. The formal scoring
method tried out in this study was not effective. At the
very best it did not improve much on an impressionistic
use of the test; at the worst it reduced rather than increased accuracy.

3 The Sentence Completion Test must be used with caution, but it can provide information which may be of considerable use in connection with a subsequent psychological
interview.

School and College Ability Test (Chapter 7)

So many of the applicants had high scores in the SCAT
that there was some concern about its effectiveness. Val-

idity was gauged by grade-point average for the two years of college work after the novitiate. The results:

1 The SCAT is as good as any such test; the correlation of the Total score with achievement was .664.

2 The group is generally quite superior in ability; their mean is 314 (Converted Score).

3 Anything below 302 seems to indicate doubtful scholastic promise, but other standardized-test scores and previous grades need to be considered also.

Study of Values (Chapter 8)

The Allport-Vernon-Lindzey Study of Values was used experimentally for a few years.

1 It did not prove useful in predicting perseverance.

2 Nevertheless, it may be helpful in vocational guidance and counseling; high scores on the Religious value scale may call attention to the possibility of a vocation to the priesthood or religious life.

3 Novices are notably high in Religious values and to an extent in Social; they are quite low in Economic.

Predictors (Chapter 9)

Because some of the background conditions discussed earlier, like motivation, and a few test factors seem to indicate a high probability of failure to persevere, a method was devised for giving due weight to these elements and combining them.

1 The method worked with two groups of subjects but not with a third.

2 But this last group is too recent to provide sound evidence, and it will be necessary to wait a little longer for an adequate test of the method.

Brothers (Chapter 10)

Only a few studies were made of candidates who wished to enter as brothers. The topics were: overall judgment of fitness, bad cases caught or missed, and the Army General Classification Test.

1 With perseverance as the criterion, the accuracy of the overall judgment of the psychologist is similar to that for the other candidates, but the data are clearer in showing that the great majority of those judged doubtful or unsatisfactory leave the religious life. From another standpoint, namely, what proportion of those who actually left had been declared doubtful or unsatisfactory, the results are also better. Fifty per cent of those who left were thus

identified, as against thirty per cent of the candidates for the priesthood.

2 In regard to the clear cases of unfitness, whether from the standpoint of mental health or other serious failures of adjustment, on the average two were caught each year and one was missed every other year. This also is a little better than the results with the other candidates.

3 The data of the AGCT show that the brothers as a group are considerably above average: their mean, which is 115.55, corresponds to about the 75th percentile for men in general and the 32nd percentile for college entrants.

4 In the case of those with an AGCT score below 100, positive evidence of ability should be sought from other sources. If the score is below 90, the chances of success are rather slight.

Appendix A

SUPPLEMENTARY INFORMATION FORMS

This appendix contains the supplementary information forms referred to in Chapter 1. The first antedates the screening program by several years and was used with the first five classes. The second was developed by the psychologist then in charge and supplanted the previous one in 1955. In as far as the writer can recall from personal communication or infer from notes in the files turned over to him, the traits were chosen partly to parallel the MMPI scales and partly from a list of significant qualities suggested by the master of novices. The third was a simplification prepared by the writer in response to complaints about the difficulty of rating many of the traits; the adjectives in the checklist were taken from the preceding form and from tentative lists drawn up by the writer and the master of novices. It was introduced in 1958. The fourth, which is the current form, was modelled after one used by the Peace Corps. It was first adapted by the staff of one superior of the Order, then further revised by the writer and the vocation directors of the superiors for whom he works.

In the use of these forms, the writer has seen little value in the ratings themselves, except insofar as they prompt comments and explanations. The recent form has been in use for two years now. One advantage that it seems to have is the provision of several spaces for explanation and documentation of the ratings. This seems to elicit more description of the candidates than was obtained by the request for a brief personality sketch, even though attention was called specifically to motivation, family background, maturity, stability, and so on.

Form I

Informatio Praevia de Candidato

De .... a ....

NOTE: In supplying this information you should not give the candidate the benefit of a doubt which may exist in your mind. What is desired is that you should record your doubt, or even better, the reasons for it. You need not fear that your mere doubts or suspicions will mean rejection of a candidate. The information which you furnish is only supplementary.

Check the column which applies to the candidate on each of the following traits.

	Deficient	*Poor*	*Average*	*Good*	*Excelle*
Dependability					
Cooperation with teachers					
General sociability with classmates					
Application to class work					
Participation in physical activities					
Participation in other extra-curricular activities					

Check the proper column on each of the following characteristi

	Clearly Yes	*Clearly No*	*Doubtful*	*No Knowledg*
1 Seclusive				
2 Moody				
3 Suspicious				
4 Effeminate				
5 Deceptive				
6 Nervous				
7 Temper displays				
8 Immature				
9 A "show-off"				
10 A "day-dreamer"				
11 "Peculiar"				

	Clearly Yes	Clearly No	Doubtful	No Knowledge

12 Asthma or hay fever
13 Tics or twitchings
14 Heart trouble
15 Stomach or bowel
   trouble
16 Fainting spells
17 Fits or convul-
   sions
18 Chronic ill health

If you have any further helpful comments on the candidate or his background, or if you wish to explain the reason for any of the above ratings, add it on the other side of this sheet and check in this square. ☐

What was the duration and nature of your contacts with this candidate? ....
Die .... Mensis .... Anni ....
Do you consider the candidate   Ita judico in Domino,
a good prospect? ....

Form II

Informatio Praevia de Candidato

De .... a ....

Indicate the pertinent characteristics of the above candidate
on a five-point scale in which 1 represents *very much*; 2, *much*;
3, *average*; 4, *some*; 5, *none*.

1	Worrisome	1 2 3 4 5		20	Self-opinionated	1 2 3 4
2	Stubborn	1 2 3 4 5		21	Scrupulous	1 2 3 4
3	Impetuous	1 2 3 4 5		22	Quarrelsome	1 2 3 4
4	"Cagey"	1 2 3 4 5		23	Love of ease	1 2 3 4
5	Diligent	1 2 3 4 5		24	"Good mixer"	1 2 3 4
6	Eccentric	1 2 3 4 5		25	Dependable	1 2 3 4
7	Boastful	1 2 3 4 5		26	Diffident	1 2 3 4
8	Cheerful	1 2 3 4 5		27	Cooperative	1 2 3 4
9	Naive	1 2 3 4 5		28	Daydreamer	1 2 3 4
10	Selfish	1 2 3 4 5		29	Show off	1 2 3 4
11	"Breezy"	1 2 3 4 5		30	Suspicious	1 2 3 4
12	Sensitive	1 2 3 4 5		31	"Lone wolf"	1 2 3 4
13	Sincere	1 2 3 4 5		32	Moody	1 2 3 4
14	Tactful	1 2 3 4 5		33	Persevering	1 2 3 4
15	"Griper"	1 2 3 4 5		34	Industrious	1 2 3 4
16	Fearful	1 2 3 4 5		35	Prone to alibi	1 2 3 4
17	Conceited	1 2 3 4 5		36	Perfectionist	1 2 3 4
18	Resentful	1 2 3 4 5		37	"Hot headed"	1 2 3 4
19	Generous	1 2 3 4 5		38	Respectful	1 2 3 4

What is his most outstanding characteristic? _____

Your impression of candidate's suitability for the religious lif
(encircle one):

Very favorable   Favorable   Doubtful   Unfavorable

On the reverse side, please give a brief personality sketch
based on your ratings, along with other pertinent material,
e.g., personal appearance, neatness, sense of humor, range
of intellectual interests, and so forth.

Form III

Informatio Praevia de Candidato

Candidate: _____   Rated by: _____

Check the characteristics you have noted in the candidate
to a significant degree, i.e., so that one would notice the
characteristic in him more than in the average young man of
his age and experience.

1	Cheerful ___	31	Opinionated ___
2	Pessimistic ___	32	Tolerant ___
3	Worrier ___	33	Cooperative ___
4	Charitable ___	34	Quarrelsome ___
5	Sarcastic ___	35	"Hotheaded" ___
6	"Griper" ___	36	Patient ___
7	Loyal ___	37	Resentful ___
8	"Touchy" ___	38	Forgiving ___
9	Suspicious ___	39	Well-balanced ___
10	Trustful ___	40	Eccentric ___
11	Courageous ___	41	Humble ___
12	Timid ___	42	Conceited ___
13	Diffident ___	43	Vain ___
14	Self-confident ___	44	Dependable ___
15	Has phobias ___	45	Daydreamer ___
16	Resourceful ___	46	Practical ___
17	Selfish ___	47	Persevering ___
18	Generous ___	48	Easily discouraged ___
19	Lazy ___	49	Moody ___
20	Diligent ___	50	Emotional ___
21	Love of ease ___	51	Stable ___
22	Mortified ___	52	Ultra-perfectionist ___
23	Impetuous ___	53	"Lone wolf" ___
24	"Cagey" ___	54	Good mixer ___
25	Open ___	55	Respectful ___
26	Sincere ___	56	Worldly ___
27	Naive ___	57	Spiritual-minded ___
28	Immature ___	58	Odd ideas ___
29	Mature ___	59	Effeminate ___
30	Stubborn ___	60	Manly ___

Your judgment of candidate's suitability for the religious
life? (Encircle one.)

Very favorable   Favorable   Doubtful   Unfavorable

Form III

In the space provided below please indicate how long you have
known the candidate, how well, and in what capacity (v.g.,
Latin teacher in Freshman year, debate coach, etc.). Then giv
a brief sketch based on your ratings, along with other pertinent facts such as family background, school history, spiritu
al development, social life, motivation, maturity, stability,
range of intellectual interests, sense of humor, and so on.
(This will be the most helpful part of your evaluation.)

Form IV

The person named above has applied for admission to the Order as a candidate for the priesthood ☐ the brotherhood ☐ . He has indicated that you among others are in a position to give us a reliable evaluation of him. I shall appreciate your thoughtful appraisal of his qualifications.

For his own welfare and happiness it is important that this young man be helped to make the right decision. Moreover the success of any religious community is in great part dependent upon the character of the candidates who are admitted. We must rely heavily on the judgment of people who know the applicant and who are willing to help us and the applicant in this important step in his life.

A candid expression of opinion is necessary. No candidate will be eliminated on the basis of a single negative rating; supporting evidence will always be obtained from other sources. All information will be kept in confidence. And we, in turn, request that you keep in confidence the fact that this young man is applying for admission to the Order. This is necessary to save him serious embarrassment if he changes his mind or is refused.

You can make a substantial contribution to the future life and happiness of the above candidate by carefully filling out and returning this form. As you will notice, the candidate has given you written permission to do so.

Sincerely yours,

Provincial

· · · · · · · · · · · · · · · · ·

This will authorize _____ to release to the above superior any and all information regarding me, together with all relevant background information.

Date _____ Signed _____

During what period have you known the candidate? _____

In what capacity have you known him, and how well? _____

☐ I do not know the applicant well enough to complete this
form.

☐ I prefer to write a letter which is attached.

COMPETENCE

Candidates for religious life should be competent. They
should be able to do a job well. In your judgment, how
competent is this candidate, as demonstrated by his work
in school or on a job?

CHECK ONE

☐ Extremely competent. Can always be counted on to do an
excellent job.

☐ Very competent.

☐ Adequate but not outstanding.

☐ Doubtful.

☐ Incompetent. Has failed on many occasions to perform
satisfactorily.

Please describe how candidate has demonstrated his level
of competence. What special skills or other assets does
the candidate have that would aid him in religious life?

EMOTIONAL MATURITY

When a person enters religious life, he experiences many
changes in ways and manners of living. He must adapt to
these changes if he is going to lead a happy and productiv
life as a religious. Keeping these considerations in mind,
how would you rate this candidate on emotional maturity
and stability and ability to tolerate stress, to work alon
or under pressure, to cope with unusual difficulties?

168

CHECK ONE

☐   SUPERB Exceptionally mature and emotionally stable. Has demonstrated his ability to function effectively in periods of stress.

☐   VERY GOOD Mature and emotionally stable.

☐   GOOD About average in emotional stability and maturity for his age group. Will need supervision.

☐   DOUBTFUL There is reason to believe that candidate will not stand up under stress.

☐   POOR Candidate is emotionally unstable, has a history of emotional outbursts, of withdrawal, of other signs of inability to cope with stress.

Comments on emotional maturity of candidate:

If any of the following are or were true of the candidate, check the item and explain below.

☐ Patient in mental hospital
☐ Nervous breakdown
☐ Under psychiatric care
☐ Under care of psychologist or social worker
☐ Required extensive counseling for emotional or behavioral problems
☐ Took frequent or extensive medication (tranquilizers, sedatives, etc.) for nervousness, anxiety, tension, or emotional disturbance
☐ Epilepsy
☐ Behavior which shows that he is not reliable, honest, or of good character
☐ Arrested, even for minor offense

Details if any of above are checked:

RELATIONSHIP WITH OTHER PEOPLE

Members of the Order work in various size groups, side by side with other religious and with lay people in a variety of tasks, sometimes in isolated areas and with minimum supervision. They work with people of all races, religions, and classes. Keeping this in mind, how would you rate this applicant on relationships with other people?

CHECK ONE   You may cross out what does not apply in the item you have checked.

☐   SUPERB   Unusually effective in relationships with others. Works well alone or in groups. Can lead or follow as occasion demands. Is regarded as a good and dependable friend. Relates well to all kinds of people, respects them and gains their respect.

☐   VERY GOOD   Works quite well with others.

☐   GOOD   About average in effectiveness of relationships with others for his age group. Will need development.

☐   DOUBTFUL   Reason to believe that he will have difficulties working with others.

☐   POOR   Cannot work effectively with others. Is uncooperative or arouses antagonism needlessly. Distracts a group from its purposes or does not carry out his obligations. A distinct liability in a team endeavor.

Comment on candidate's relationships with other people:

SOME GENERAL FACTORS

Please comment on the following in the candidate's regard, to the extent that you can: home and family life, social development, spiritual development, motivation for the religious life, firmness of his decision to embrace religious life, the presence or absence of good judgment.

Please add any significant information or impression which has not been brought out by the preceding questions.

OVERALL RECOMMENDATION

☐ I recommend the candidate without reservation as an excellent prospect.

☐ I have some reservations but would recommend the candidate as a good prospect.

☐ I have substantial doubts about the candidate but think
   he might be given a chance to prove himself during the
   training period of the novitiate prior to final acceptance.

☐ I doubt his suitability and do not recommend admission
   of the candidate.

☐ I feel the candidate is unsuited for the religious life.

☐ Other:

_____
Signature   Title   Date

Appendix B

ITEMS IN THE REGULAR SCALES CHANGED
IN BIER'S 1955 VERSION OF THE MMPI.
SOME EXPERIMENTAL SCALES.
SOME INFORMAL DATA.

The 1955 revision of the MMPI for use in seminaries was
printed by Bier, with the permission of the publishers, for
private use. It may be distributed to others on condition
it be used for research.

The following lists are drawn up for the benefit of those
who use the seminary form and may wish to correct their stencils or prepare new ones. Hence, the numbers refer to Bier's
1955 version or, if you will, to the answer sheet.

L Scale: Delete: 15, 45, 285.

K: No deletions. Add the following, which originally
were found after #366: 14-F, 45-F, 49-F, 50-F, 113-F, 184-
F, 258-F. (In the key for the back of the answer sheet, all
except the first two holes are for items originally after
366 and are ignored.)

F: So many have been changed that it is simpler to make
an entirely new key. The following are the items *retained*:
31-T, 34-T, 35-T, 40-T, 42-T, 48-T, 54-F, 56-T, 65-F, 66-
T, 75-F, 83-F, 85-T, 112-F, 121-T, 123-T, 139-T, 146-T, 151-
T, 156-T, 164-F, 168-T, 169-F, 185-F, 196-F, 197-T, 200-T,

202-T, 209-T, 210-T, 211-T, 218-T, 220-F, 227-T, 245-T, 246-
T, 247-T, 252-T, 256-T, 257-F, 269-T, 272-F, 275-T, 276-F,
286-T, 288-T, 291-T, 293-T.

Hs: No change.

D: Delete: 58-F, 95-F, 98-F, 208-F, 285-F.

Hy: No change.

Pd: Delete: 20-F, 37-F, 38-T, 215-T, 231-F.

Mf (males): Delete: 70-T, 74-T, 115-F, 133-F, 231-T,
249-F.

Pa: Delete: 27-T, 314-T.

Pt: Delete: 15-T.

Sc: Delete: 15-T, 17-F, 177-F, 302-F, 310-F, 311-T.

Ma: Delete: 11-T, 101-F, 167-T.

Si: Fortunately, several of the items after 366 were
transferred to earlier positions. It is simpler to list
all the items *retained*: 17-F, 25-F, 32-T, 33-F, 45-T, 57-
F, 67-T, 82-T, 91-F, 98-F, 99-F, 111-T, 113-T, 117-T, 119-
F, 124-T, 126-F, 138-T, 143-F, 147-T, 167-T, 171-T, 172-
T, 177-F, 180-T, 193-F, 199-T, 201-T, 208-F, 229-F, 236-
T, 254-F, 262-F, 267-T, 278-T, 281-F, 285-F, 292-T, 296-
F, 304-T, 309-F, 316-T, 321-T, 332-T, 336-T, 342-T, 353-
F, 357-T, 359-F.

B: All are scored T. 6, 12, 69, 77, 79, 91, 93, 99,
100, 102, 109, 111, 136, 141, 162, 165, 166, 181, 232,
240, 244, 248, 254, 255, 264, 270, 280, 292, 298, 304,
319, 321, 329, 340, 361. (Measures response bias, or tendency to say "yes." Fricke, cf. Dahlstrom and Welsh, 1960,
pp. 113, 450.)

C: 6-T, 30-T, 37-T, 56-T, 67-T, 80-F, 92-F, 96-F,
105-T, 111-F, 116-T, 134-T, 145-T, 162-T, 169-T, 174-F,
181-T, 220-F, 225-T, 236-T, 238-T, 242-F, 250-F, 285-T,
291-F, 296-T, 313-F, 319-T, 337-T, 360-F. (Control Scale
designated Cn by Cuadra. Note that the scoring is in the
reverse direction from that of the others; low scores are
better than high. The <u>T</u> scores in the writer's norms have
been reversed to make high scores undesirable as in the
other MMPI scales. #56, 96, and 220 were omitted in the
writer's keys. Cuadra, cf. Dahlstrom and Welsh, pp. 120,
301, 451.)

A: All are scored T except for #58, as indicated:
15, 20, 32, 37, 41, 45, 49, 50, <u>58-F</u>, 67, 76, 94, 138, 147,
205, 236, 259, 267, 278, 301, 305, 321, 337, 343, 344, 345,
356, 359. (Welsh's first factor, anxiety. Cf. Dahlstrom
and Welsh, pp. 84 f., 448.)

R: All are scored F: 1, 6, 9, 12, 39, 51, 81, 95, 98,
112, 126, 131, 140, 145, 154, 156, 184, 191, 208, 219, 221,
231, 258, 271, 272, 281, 282, 327. Only the last one is on
the back side of the answer sheet; the reader may wish to
drop this, but he will have to change the norms. (Welsh's

second factor, repression. Cf. Dahlstrom and Welsh, pp. 84 f., 464.)

SD: 7-T, 18-T, 32-F, 40-F, 42-F, 43-F, 45-F, 54-T, 107-T, 138-F, 148-F, 156-F, 158-F, 163-T, 169-T, 171-F, 186-F, 218-F, 241-F, 245-F, 247-F, 252-F, 257-T, 263-F, 267-F, 269-F, 286-F, 301-F, 321-F, 335-F, 337-F, 352-F. (Called So-r by Dahlstrom and Welsh; social desirability, i.e., the response professes behavior of a socially desirable sort. Edwards, 1957; cf. Dahlstrom and Welsh, pp. 111 f., 466.)

Se (or Re): 11-F, 18-F, 21-T, 32-T, 36-F, 41-T, 46-F, 56-T, 57-F, 61-T, 67-T, 68-F, 72-T, 77-T, 78-T, 82-T, 86-T, 91-F, 96-F, 102-T, 107-F, 108-T, 111-F, 119-F, 130-F, 139-T, 142-T, 147-T, 152-F, 158-T, 160-F, 163-F, 164-F, 167-T, 171-T, 172-T, 179-T, 188-F, 193-F, 199-T, 201-T, 205-T, 207-F, 217-T, 224-T, 226-T, 232-F, 237-T, 244-T, 259-T, 260-T, 261-F, 267-T, 274-F, 278-T, 294-F, 297-T, 299-T, 301-T, 305-T, 309-F, 317-T, 321-T, 336-T, 337-T, 349-T, 353-F, 356-T, 357-T, 361-T. (Seminary, or Religious Scale, as revised by the writer. Barry, 1960; Coelho, 1963.)

Wa: 3-F, 9-F, 13-T, 16-T, 32-T, 35-T, 40-T, 41-T, 53-F, 59-T, 84-T, 88-F, 109-T, 112-T, 164-F, 167-T, 170-T, 184-T, 207-F, 244-T, 250-T, 257-F, 259-T, 272-T, 301-T, 312-T, 318-F, 335-T, 343-T. (#272 was answered T by all but one of the 85 subjects; the items on the back side of the answer sheet may not contribute much: about three-fourths of the good group had zero scores on this side, and about half of the poor group. Tydlaska and Mengel, 1953; cf. Dahlstrom and Welsh, p. 468.)

Id: 5-T, 6-T, 9-F, 19-T, 25-T, 28-T, 32-T, 33-T, 36-F, 41-T, 43-T, 46-F, 55-F, 61-T, 76-T, 93-T, 96-F, 100-T, 102-T, 113-T, 118-T, 122-F, 124-T, 145-T, 184-T, 186-T, 213-T, 223-T, 224-T, 225-F, 230-F, 234-T, 238-T, 239-T, 242-F, 243-F, 247-T, 251-T, 253-F, 272-F, 280-T, 291-T, 294-F, 303-T, 306-F, 312-T, 316-T, 317-T, 330-F, 338-T, 344-T, 347-F, 364-T. (Irregular medical discharge. Calden, Thurston, Stewart, and Vineberg; cf. Dahlstrom and Welsh, pp. 354, 457.)

N: 2-F, 3-F, 6-T, 9-F, 29-T, 41-T, 43-T, 44-T, 46-F, 47-T, 51-F, 68-F, 72-T, 76-T, 103-F, 107-F, 108-T, 114-T, 159-T, 175-F, 178-F, 186-T, 189-T, 190-F, 191-T, 236-T, 238-T, 242-F, 283-T. (Called Ne by Dahlstrom and Welsh; neuroticism. Winne, 1951; cf. Dahlstrom and Welsh, p. 461.)

Bier: 3-F, 5-T, 13-T, 32-T, 36-F, 41-T, 62-T, 67-T, 79-F, 86-T, 94-T, 106-T, 128-F, 138-T, 142-T, 152-F, 160-F, 163-F, 165-F, 170-F, 172-T, 179-T, 186-T, 190-F, 198-F, 217-T, 236-T, 238-T, 241-T, 287-F, 301-T, 317-T, 321-T, 335-T, 352-T, 356-T, 357-T, 361-T. (Listed by Bier, 1948, as discriminating between the well-adjusted and poorly adjusted seminarians, but nature of response was not indicated. The present writer determined the direction of scoring on *a priori* grounds. Bier, 1948, p. 68.)

Es: 2-F, 15-T, 22-T, 32-T, 33-T, 34-T, 36-F, 43-T, 48-T, 51-F, 62-T, 70-T, 82-T, 94-T, 100-T, 109-F, 132-T, 140-T, 153-F, 174-F, 181-F, 187-F, 189-T, 192-F, 209-T, 217-T, 221-F, 234-F, 236-T, 241-T, 244-T, 251-T, 253-F, 261-T, 270-F, 341-T, 344-T, 349-T, 355-F, 359-T. (Ego strength. Scoring reversed from Barron's in order to conform to general trend of MMPI scores. Barron; cf. Dahlstrom and Welsh, pp. 301 f., 356, 454.)

Hsx: 4-T, 18-T, 33-T, 37-F, 118-F, 129-F, 132-T, 162-F, 166-T, 171-T, 205-F, 217-F, 219-F, 241-F, 295-T. (Homosexuality. Panton, 1960.)

Critical items: 13 (290), 16 (315), 24 (333), 31, 32 (328), 33 (323), 35 (331), 36, 40, 48, 53, 61, 65, 66, 69, 73, 76, 79, 85, 96, 104, 107, 110, 121, 123, 131, 136, 137, 139, 146, 151, 154, 156, 158, 167, 168, 179, 182, 194, 197, 198, 199, 200, 202, 209, 212, 213, 216, 220, 224, 226, 227, 239, 241, 245, 247, 250, 251, 266, 275, 291, 293, 294, 301, 320, 334, 337, 339, 341, 346, 347, 349, 350, 355, 360, 364. And perhaps add: 97, 238, 345. (*Not* derived from the critical item list of Grayson. Cf. Dahlstrom and Welsh, pp. 434 f. Not used as a scale, but examined and then checked in interview.)

Peterson's Signs: (1) Four or more scores over 70 in clinical scales. (2) F greater than 65. (3) Sc greater than Pt. (4) Pa or Ma greater than 70. (5) Pa or Sc or Ma greater than Hs and D and Hy. (6) D greater than Hs and Hy. One point is allowed for each sign, and cutting score is above 1 or 2. Diagnosis is presence or absence of psychosis (schizophrenia in Peterson's study). With either cutting score 74 per cent of the diagnoses are reported to be correct. In the writer's experience, the signs do not work with seminary candidates. (Welsh and Dahlstrom, 1956, pp. 415-18; Dahlstrom and Welsh, p. 286.)

The experimental scales indicated above and a number of indices were tried from time to time and found of little or no help, except as indicated in Chapter 3. The criterion was usually perseverance. These studies are merely mentioned here for the information of the reader, without supporting data. Usually they were done with one, two, or three classes.

The measures used with Bier's 1949 version were:

1 Range of $\underline{T}$ scores among the clinical scales, except Mf: i.e., the highest $\underline{T}$ score minus the lowest.
2 Mf spike: i.e., Mf the highest and at a $\underline{T}$ score of 70 or more.

3   Subtle and Obvious scales for D, Hy, Pd, Pa, Ma (Wiener; Welsh and Dahlstrom, pp. 195-204.)
4   Sum of <u>T</u> scores on Pd and Ma, both with K correction.
5   B score.
6   Ma of 20 or more (raw score).
7   Ma of 20 or more and B of 17 or more (both raw scores).
8   Id, Irregular Discharge.
9   N, Neuroticism.
10 Bier Scale. (As indicated in preceding section. The attempt to use these items as a scale was the writer's doing, against Bier's advice.)

The measures used with the 1955 version were:

1   Ma of 20 or more (raw score).
2   Es, Ego Strength.
3   Peterson's signs. (As indicated in preceding section.)
4   Hsx, Homosexuality. (Found to be useless for our purposes.)

The following are some correlations involving experimental and regular scales, all based on one year's applicants numbering 53:

K and SD: .636
B and L: -.675
B and Pd: -.262

References

For convenience, references are given to Dahlstrom and Welsh rather than the original articles whenever the description in this handbook is reasonably sufficient. References are not repeated here if they have been given in Chapter 3, except for the two books by Dahlstrom and Welsh.

Dahlstrom, W. Grant, and Welsh, George S. *An MMPI Handbook: A Guide to Use in Clinical Practice and Research*. Minneapolis: University of Minnesota Press, 1960.
Panton, James H. A new MMPI scale for the identification of homosexuality. *J. clin. Psychol.*, 1960, 16, 17-21.
Welsh, George S., and Dahlstrom, W. Grant (Eds.) *Basic Readings on the MMPI in Psychology and Medicine*. Minneapolis: University of Minnesota Press, 1956.
Winne, John F. A scale of neuroticism: an adaptation of the Minnesota Multiphasic Personality Inventory. *J. clin. Psychol.*, 1951, 7, 117-22.

SEMINARY NORMS FOR THE MMPI

Norms for Bier's 1955 modification of the MMPI, based on 297 applicants for a religious order of men, 1956-1959. The K correction is not used.

Linear T Scores

T Scores

Raw Score	L	F	K	Hs	D	Hy	Pd	Mf	Pa	Pt	Sc	Ma	Si	Raw Score
48								101					109	48
47								99					108	47
46								96					106	46
45								94					104	45
44								92					102	44
43							112	90					101	43
42							109	87					99	42
41							107	85					97	41

Raw Score	L	F	K	Hs	D	Hy	Pd	Mf	Pa	Pt	Sc	Ma	Si	Raw Score
40					104			83					95	40
39					101			81					94	39
38					98			78		111			92	38
37					95			76		109		110	90	37
36					93			74		107		108	88	36
35				113	90			72		105		105	87	35
34				109	87			69		103	112	102	85	34
33				106	84			67		101	110	100	83	33
32				103	81	111		65		99	107	97	81	32
31				100	79	108		62		97	105	94	80	31
30			80	97	76	104		60		95	103	92	78	30
29			77	94	73	101		58		93	101	89	76	29
28			75	90	70	98		56		91	98	86	74	28
27			72	87	67	94		53		89	96	83	73	27
26			70	84	65	91		51		87	94	81	71	26
25			67	81	62	88		49		85	91	78	69	25
24			65	78	59	84		47		83	89	75	67	24
23			62	74	56	81		44	110	81	87	73	66	23
22			60	71	53	78		42	106	79	84	70	64	22
21			58	68	51	74		40	102	77	82	67	62	21
20			55	65	48	71		38	97	75	80	65	60	20
19			53	62	45	68		35	93	73	77	62	59	19
18			50	112	59	42	64	33	89	71	75	59	57	18
17			48	108	55	39	61	31	84	69	73	56	55	17
16			45	104	52	37	58	29	80	67	71	54	53	16
15			43	100	49	34	54	26	76	65	68	51	51	15
14			40	95	46	31	51	24	72	63	66	48	50	14
13			38	91	43	28	48	22	67	61	64	46	48	13
12	93		36	87	39	25	44	20	63	59	61	43	46	12
11	88	112	33	83	36	23	41	17	59	57	59	40	44	11
10	83	105	31	79	33	20	38	15	54	55	57	38	43	10
9	78	99	28	75	30	17	34	13	50	53	54	35	41	9
8	73	92	26	71	27	14	31	10	46	51	52	32	39	8
7	68	85	23	67	23	11	28		41	49	50	30	37	7
6	63	78	21	63	20	9	24		37	47	48	27	36	6
5	58	72	18	59	17		21		33	45	45	24	34	5
4	53	65	16	55	14		18		29	43	43	21	32	4
3	48	58	14	50	11		14		24	41	41	19	30	3
2	43	51	11	46			11		20	39	38	16	29	2
1	38	45		42					16	37	36	13	27	1
0	33	38		38					11	35	34	11	25	0

T Scores

Raw Score	B	C	A	R	SD
48					
47					
46					
45					
44					
43					
42					
41					
40					
39					
38					
37	112				
36	109				
35	106				
34	104				
33	101				
32	99				63
31	96				59
30	94				56
29	91		111		52
28	89		109	106	48
27	86		106	103	45
26	84	10	103	99	41
25	81	14	101	96	37
24	78	17	98	92	34
23	76	20	96	89	30
22	73	24	93	86	26
21	71	27	90	82	23
20	68	31	88	79	19
19	66	34	85	75	16
18	63	37	83	72	12
17	61	41	80	69	
16	58	44	78	65	
15	56	48	75	62	
14	53	51	72	58	
13	50	54	70	55	
12	48	58	67	52	
11	45	61	65	48	

T Scores

Raw Score	B	C	A	R	SD
10	43	64	62	45	
9	40	68	59	41	
8	38	71	57	38	
7	35	75	54	34	
6	33	78	52	31	
5	30	81	49	28	
4	28	85	46	24	
3	25	88	44	21	
2	22	92	41	17	
1	20	95	39	14	
0	17	98	36	11	

Scale	Mean	Standard Deviation
L	3.39	2.00
F	1.80	1.48
K	17.91	4.09
Hs	2.88	2.45
D	15.33	3.14
Hy	20.78	3.57
Pd	13.69	3.01
Mf	25.47	4.42
Pa	8.99	2.32
Pt	7.61	4.97
Sc	7.07	4.34
Ma	14.60	3.71
Si	14.15	5.69
B	12.82	3.93
C	14.26	2.95
A	5.40	3.85
R	11.56	2.94
SD	28.48	2.75

Normalized <u>T</u> Scores

<u>T</u> Scores

Raw Score	L	F	K	Hs	D	Hy	Pd	Mf	Pa	Pt	Sc	Ma	Si	Raw Score
39								79						39
38								78						38
37								75						37
36								71						36
35								69					79	35
34								67					78	34
33								66					78	33
32								65					76	32
31						79		63					74	31
30						75		61					72	30
29						72		59					71	29
28					79	70		56					70	28
27			79		78	68		53					70	27
26			73		76	65		51		79			68	26
25			70		75	62		49		79	78	79	67	25
24			65		75	59		47		78	78	78	66	24
23			62		73	56	78	45		76	78	72	64	23
22			59		70	53	73	43		75	76	68	63	22
21			56		67	50	71	40		72	73	66	62	21
20			54		64	47	68	38		70	71	64	61	20
19			52		61	45	65	35		69	71	61	59	19
18			51		58	42	64	32		68	70	58	57	18
17			48		56	40	62	30		67	69	56	56	17
16			45		53	38	59	27		65	67	54	54	16
15			43		50	35	55	22	75	63	66	52	53	15
14			41		46	32	52	21	70	62	65	49	51	14
13			38	79	43	28	48		67	60	64	46	49	13
12			36	78	39	22	44		63	59	61	43	47	12
11			34	75	35		41		58	58	59	40	46	11
10	78		32	72	31		38		54	56	57	38	44	10
9	73		29	70	27		33		50	54	56	34	42	9
8	70	79	26	67	24		30		46	52	54	30	38	8
7	66	76	22	65	21		27		41	50	51	28	35	7
6	62	73		62			21		37	48	49	26	32	6
5	58	68		59					33	46	47	21	30	5
4	54	63		56					29	44	44		25	4
3	49	59		52					22	42	41			3
2	44	53		48						38	36			2
1	37	46		43						33	29			1
0	29	37		36						26				0

T Scores

Raw Score	B	C	A	R	SD
39					
38					
37					
36					
35					
34					
33					
32					66
31					59
30					54
29					50
28					46
27					44
26					41
25	79				38
24	78				36
23	78				33
22	74				31
21	70	26			28
20	67	31	79	76	26
19	65	35	76	72	22
18	62	38	75	71	
17	60	41	74	68	
16	58	45	71	64	
15	56	48	69	61	
14	54	51	68	58	
13	51	54	67	55	
12	48	57	66	52	
11	46	61	64	49	
10	43	64	61	45	
9	40	68	59	42	
8	37	72	57	38	
7	35	76	55	32	
6	33		53	29	
5	30		51	26	
4	27		48	22	
3	22		45	21	
2			42		
1			37		
0			30		

Appendix D

FIRST VERSION OF SENTENCE COMPLETION TEST
(Courtesy of Rev. William C. Bier, S.J.,
Fordham University)

SENTENCE COMPLETION TEST

Name _____ Date _____

Instructions: Complete the following sentences. Be sure to
make a complete sentence. Do not omit any. Work rapidly.

1 I feel that a real friend _____
2 When the odds are against me _____
3 I would do anything to forget the time I _____
4 If I were in charge _____
5 To me the future looks _____
6 People whom I consider my superiors _____
7 I know it is silly, but I am afraid of _____
8 My father hardly ever _____
9 When I was a child _____
10 My ideal of a woman is _____
11 In working I get along best with _____
12 My feeling about married life is _____

```
13  Most of all I want to _____
14  Compared with most families, mine _____
15  I don't like people who _____
16  My mother _____
17  I believe that I have the ability to _____
18  My greatest mistake was _____
19  If people work for me _____
20  Ten years from now, I _____
21  In my school, my teachers _____
22  Most of my friends don't know that I was afraid of _____
23  If my father would only _____
24  I was never happier than _____
25  I think most girls _____
26  My fellow students _____
27  Most families I know _____
28  I think a wife should _____
29  I could be happy if _____
30  My mother and I _____
31  The people I like best _____
32  My greatest weakness is _____
33  At times I have felt ashamed _____
34  I wish that I were in charge of _____
35  Some day I _____
36  When I see the person in charge coming _____
37  I wish I could lose the fear of _____
38  Compared with my mother, my dad _____
39  My most vivid childhood memory _____
40  What I like least about women _____
41  My family treats me like _____
42  I like working with people who _____
43  When I feel sexual impulses _____
44  My mother thinks that my father _____
45  My secret ambition in life _____
46  When I am not around, my friends _____
47  Compared with others, I _____
48  I feel particularly guilty about _____
49  In giving orders to others, I _____
50  I look forward to _____
51  I can work best when my supervisor _____
52  My fears sometimes force me to _____
53  My father and I _____
54  I remember when _____
55  When I think of women _____
56  When I was a child my family _____
57  I feel that sex is _____
58  I think that most mothers _____
59  People who work with me usually _____
60  What I want out of life _____
```

183

BACKGROUND INFORMATION FORM
(For use with aptitude tests for brothers)

Name _____ Age _____ Date _____
                                Date of birth _____

Education

School	Name of school	Completed Last grade	Date (year)	Type of course
Elementary				
High				
College				
Vocational				

Subjects liked most: _____
Subjects liked least: _____
Best grades in: _____
Poorest grades in: _____

184

How well did you like school? _____ If starting over,
would you choose the same line of study? _____
Was your last year's scholastic standing low? _____ below
average? _____ average? _____ above average? _____
high? _____
If your education has been cut off before completion, why?
_____

Has school study been easy? _____ fairly easy? _____
difficult? _____ very difficult? _____
What training or courses taken do you consider most valuable
to you? _____
In what fields of learning are you best informed? _____
_____
In what extracurricular activities were you active? _____
_____
What achievements in school gave you great satisfaction?
_____

Experience and Job Preferences

List previous work you have done, including part-time
work and any government or armed service. Put first job
last.

Job or position	Date (year) Began	Left	Weekly Wage	How liked?	Why Left?

Which of the above jobs did you like best? _____
Why? _____
Which of the above did you like least? _____
Why? _____
Have you any type of operational license or degree? _____
In this list of occupations, check those you think you would
like:

Accounting & bookkeeping ___
Agriculture ___
Baking ___
Brick & stone laying ___
Buyer & purchasing agent ___
Cabinet making ___
Carpentering ___
Clerical ___
Clothes keeper ___

Cooking ___
Domestic service ___
Electrical ___
Engineering, boiler ___
Food & home economics ___
Gardening & grounds-
keeping ___
Infirmarian ___
Janitor ___

Laundering ___　　　　　　　　Plumbing ___
Machinist ___　　　　　　　　Porter ___
Mail handling ___　　　　　　Sacristan ___
Maintenance, automobiles ___　Secretarial ___
Maintenance, building ___　　Shoe repair ___
Maintenance, machines ___　　Stenographic ___
Mechanical ___　　　　　　　Tailoring ___
Painting, house ___

In what kind of activities, work, etc., do you feel that you
are not very good? (For example: music, sports, clerical
work, mathematics) _____
_____

In which do you feel that you are good? _____
_____

What are your greatest vocational assets (qualities, special
abilities, skills, etc.) as you see them? _____
_____

List three to six occupations in which you think you could be
happy, in order of preference:
1 _____　　4 _____
2 _____　　5 _____
3 _____　　6 _____

Other Interests and Traits

Present hobbies and keen interests: _____
_____

Past hobbies or interests (if different): _____
_____

Clubs or organizations you belonged to: _____
_____

In what activities have you taken a leading part? _____
_____

Did you participate in sports? ____ sing? ____ paint? ____
write? ____ draw? ____ play musical instruments? ___
read much? ____
What did you enjoy more than anything else? _____
What magazines did you habitually read? _____
_____

What sort of books did you like to read? _____
_____
_____

List four or five of your prominent character traits:
　　Assets or strong points　　　Hindrances or weak points

　　_____　　_____
　　_____　　_____
　　_____　　_____

Health

Physical condition: excellent? ____ good? ____ fair? ____
poor? ____
Physical handicaps or health difficulties that bother you:
_____
What do you do to keep in good physical condition? _____
_____
Are you able to relax easily after strenuous effort? _____
_____
Date of last complete physical examination? _____
Result? _____
When did you last visit a doctor? _____
Why? _____
Do you sleep as well as most people? _____
Is your digestion as good as that of most people? _____
Vision without glasses? _____ with glasses? _____

Comments

Write here any comments or explanations you think will be of
help: